Stop Procrastinating and Get Things Done

Adrian Tannock

Adrian Tannock is an experienced therapist and author specializing in emotional and behavioural difficulties. Aside from his work as a therapist, Adrian also works with professional athletes to help improve their performance. As a result, he holds a particular interest in confidence and motivation.

Adrian is a passionate writer. His other books include: Teach Yourself *Beat Insomnia with NLP* (Hodder, 2011) and *The Teach Yourself Confidence Workbook* (Hodder, 2012). Outside of work, his interests include staying fit, studying and volunteer work. His therapy practice is based in Manchester, UK.

For Sian Schofield, whose support has proved invaluable.

Teach® Yourself

Stop Procrastinating and Get Things Done

Adrian Tannock

Hodder Education

338 Euston Road, London NW1 3BH

Hodder Education is an Hachette UK company

First published in UK 2012 by Hodder Education

First published in US 2012 by The McGraw-Hill Companies, Inc.

Copyright © 2012 Adrian Tannock

The moral rights of the author have been asserted.

Database right Hodder Education (makers)

The *Teach Yourself* name is a registered trademark of Hachette UK.

British Library Cataloguing in Publication Data: a catalogue record for this title is available from the British Library.

Library of Congress Catalog Card Number: on file.

10 9 8 7 6 5 4 3 2 1

The publisher has used its best endeavours to ensure that any website addresses referred to in this book are correct and active at the time of going to press. However, the publisher and the author have no responsibility for the websites and can make no guarantee that a site will remain live or that the content will remain relevant, decent or appropriate.

The publisher has made every effort to mark as such all words which it believes to be trademarks. The publisher should also like to make it clear that the presence of a word in the book, whether marked or unmarked, in no way affects its legal status as a trademark.

Every reasonable effort has been made by the publisher to trace the copyright holders of material in this book. Any errors or omissions should be notified in writing to the publisher, who will endeavour to rectify the situation for any reprints and future editions.

Hachette UK's policy is to use papers that are natural, renewable and recyclable products and made from wood grown in sustainable forests. The logging and manufacturing processes are expected to conform to the environmental regulations of the country of origin.

Cover image © babimu – Fotolia

www.hoddereducation.co.uk

Typeset by Cenveo Publisher Services

Printed in Great Britain by CPI Group (UK) Ltd, Croydon, CR0 4YY

Also available in ebook

Acknowledgements

A special thanks to Hannah Gray. I could not have completed this manuscript without her patient help.

Contents

Understanding procrastination

In this chapter you will learn:

- ► *What is meant by procrastination and how it can seriously damage your life, your career and personal relationships*
- ► *How procrastination is in fact a process – a series of decisions not to do something even if this is unconscious*
- ► *How to begin to address your own procrastination by analysing the areas of your life – job, home life, relationships, health and so on – where it is a problem*
- ► *How to use this book.*

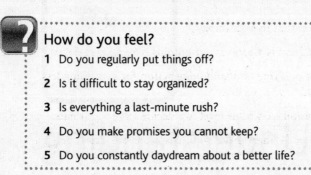

How do you feel?

1 Do you regularly put things off?

2 Is it difficult to stay organized?

3 Is everything a last-minute rush?

4 Do you make promises you cannot keep?

5 Do you constantly daydream about a better life?

As you may already be aware, you are not a robot. You may yearn to be perfectly motivated but the truth is more complicated than that.

Some people *do* push themselves to the limits, and this can be positive. Olympic athletes endure punishing regimes to compete at the pinnacle of their sport. Such single-minded determination can also be destructive. Consider the workaholic whose children grow up without them. Abundant determination is only positive when applied to your best interests.

You have bought this book – or it has been bought for you – because you struggle with *procrastination*. Step by step you will learn how to focus on your goals and strengthen your motivation. Overcoming procrastination is not easy, but it can be done.

In this chapter, we will explore procrastination in more detail: what it is, how we do it, and how it can be changed. Then we will look at how procrastination affects *your* life. So, let's start with a definition.

What is procrastination?

Read through the following definition:

> Procrastination happens *before or during a task*, when we *take the decision*, for no *valid* reason, to *delay* or *abandon* that task in favour of something *less important* – despite knowing there will be *negative consequences* as a result.

This definition tells us four things:

1 Procrastination is a *process* – it unfolds over several stages.

2 It involves *delaying* or *abandoning* action for something less important.

3 It is a *decision* – on some level, we decide to procrastinate.

4 It is *irrational* – there is no valid reason for our delay, and we know it will lead to negative consequences.

Procrastination is deeply frustrating. At its worst, it ruins lives. There is rarely a single cause, and rarely a single solution. To understand this fully, let's look at the stages of procrastination in more detail.

The procrastination process

▶ **Stage 1 – before or during a task.** Procrastination halts *action*. We can procrastinate over anything – including pleasurable experiences (e.g. reading or going to the cinema), and even activities like using the toilet or going to sleep.

▶ **Stage 2 – taking a decision.** To delay or abandon a task, we *have* to make a decision. Often, this happens quickly – a habitual or semi-conscious thought that barely registers.

▶ **Stage 3 – justifying the decision.** If we thought only rationally, we would never procrastinate – our logic would not allow it. Instead, we *excuse* our decision, despite the negative consequences we will face.

▶ **Stage 4 – doing something less important.** What do you do when you procrastinate? Some people watch TV or socialize. Others busy themselves with 'important' tasks. For some, procrastination equates to being stuck; they daydream and fantasize about the future, or even just stare into space. *Procrastination activities* take many forms.

▶ **Stage 5 – knowing there will be negative consequences.** Despite our pretence, we know procrastination will make matters worse – and we feel powerless to stop it.

▶ **Stage 6 – experiencing the negative consequences.**
Procrastination leads to anxiety, guilt, letting people down
(including yourself), and missed opportunities. Negative
thoughts and behaviour become entrenched, making
procrastination even more likely in future.

These six stages can unfold with lightning speed. We often
fail to notice our decision to procrastinate, and instead pay
attention to our excuses. It is difficult to stop because it is so
automatic.

Everyone procrastinates at some point. It cannot be banished
completely, but debilitating procrastination can be challenged.
The first step is to accept that procrastination is a problem –
one which you cannot easily control.

Quick fix: No one's perfect

Think about people you know and admire: good friends, your partner, your
boss(!), certain celebrities or famous athletes.

Then, realize these people *are not perfect*. Even the most motivated
people procrastinate from time to time. In fact, you may already know
someone with a serious procrastination problem (although, like yourself,
they are likely to keep it secret).

Remember, everyone has their difficulties in life. Procrastination is much
more common than you think.

Although it is difficult to change, there is hope – we can
improve our focus, our motivation and our resilience. Even
when procrastination feels deeply entrenched, nothing is set
in stone.

Next, let's look at procrastination in a real-life setting.

Case study: Mike's story

Mike had struggled with procrastination for many years. He did very well
at school, but found university difficult. Mike lost his self-confidence and
started to procrastinate.

In the years since, it had become crippling. Work wasn't too much of a problem – his procrastination was curtailed by daily team meetings. Although this was stressful, he was secretly glad of this.

Mike's personal life was a different story. Relationships had ended because of his procrastination, and his flat was *always* a mess. Cleaning his kitchen was a significant problem, even though he had invested in a dishwasher. Several days would pass before he 'got around to' using it.

Here is Mike's procrastination process in full:

Step 1 – before loading the dishwasher. Mike viewed the pile of dirty dishes in his kitchen with *reluctance*. He believed the job would be unpleasant and take for ever.

Step 2 – taking the decision to avoid loading the dishwasher. Because he overstated the difficulty of the task, Mike decided to avoid it. Initially, this decision would be fleeting and semiconscious. Mike became *more aware* of his procrastination – and much less happy with it – as the dishes stacked up.

Step 3 – justifying the decision. Looking at the pile of dirty dishes, he would think: 'I don't need to do it yet...' This *procrastination excuse* barely registered, especially at first. As the dirty dishes took over his kitchen, the excuses grew more conscious and desperate: 'I know I need to do them, just not yet...' Eventually, Mike felt he had two voices in his mind – one pleading with him to load the dishwasher, and the other determined to avoid it.

Step 4 – doing something less important. After deciding to procrastinate, Mike would busy himself with 'procrastination activities': watching TV, browsing the Internet, reading, or just lazing around.

Step 5 – knowing there will be negative consequences. As the dishes mounted, his procrastination became more guilt-ridden. He would feel too stressed to watch TV or go online, and would just stare distractedly into space while thinking about loading the dishwasher.

Step 6 – experiencing the negative consequences of his procrastination. When all of Mike's dishes were dirty, he would get angry and frustrated. The negative consequences were twofold: picking through dirty dishes felt humiliating, and he hated himself for allowing things to get into such a mess.

Eventually Mike would get his act together and clean his kitchen – but not without unnecessary stress and upset. Life would be so much easier without procrastination, but as you know – the *logical truth* is not part of this story.

Mike's procrastination started at university, and then insinuated itself into another area of his life – keeping a clean and tidy home. When we learn to procrastinate, it can spread like a virus.

Also note: Mike's decision to procrastinate came before the excuse. This is usually the case. On some level, perhaps beyond our conscious awareness, we decide to delay first – and *then* the excuses come. Our excuses do not cause procrastination, they justify and reinforce it.

Mythbuster: Laziness

It would be easy to judge Mike for procrastinating: 'You're just lazy! Stop moping around, and clean your kitchen!' So, what do we mean when we describe someone as lazy?

The dictionary defines 'lazy' as being: *averse or disinclined to work*. In Mike's case, this is technically true. However, the world 'lazy' is not neutral – it is a pejorative expression of our disapproval. An insult.

Worse still, lazy is an 'umbrella term'. It strips away the complexity of procrastination, leaving us with a meaningless emotional judgement. There is much more to procrastination than simple laziness.

Do you judge yourself for procrastinating? Wouldn't it be better to accept it as a part of your life, and resolve to change it? Emotional self-judgement counts for very little; it just makes matters worse.

When do we procrastinate?

We can procrastinate at any time. You can learn to guard against it by recognizing when you are *at risk*. There are five key moments to consider, as Mike's case history demonstrates.

1 BEFORE A TASK, BUT NOT FOCUSING ON IT

Arriving home from work, Mike switches on the TV and grabs his laptop. He ignores the pile of dirty dishes in his kitchen for as long as possible. The task might need doing, but he tries not to think about it.

At this stage, we procrastinate by ignoring what needs to be done – a form of 'denial'. We excel at putting things out of our minds. The task will soon be forgotten, at least for the time being.

2 BEFORE A TASK, AND NOW FOCUSING ON IT
After a while, Mike starts to feel hungry. Looking at his dirty kitchen, he now has a decision to make: 'Should I do it now?' Consciously, Mike believes he is assessing whether to tackle the kitchen. Unconsciously, Mike has already decided he will not yet load the dishwasher. Instead, he excuses himself from taking action: 'I'm not hungry yet – I'll do it later.'

Sometimes we procrastinate by excusing ourselves from taking action, before quickly focusing elsewhere. Alternatively, we can agonize over whether to act – endlessly planning or fantasizing about taking action.

3 STARTING THE TASK
Eventually Mike feels ravenous, so he starts to load the dishwasher. He quickly finds the job too frustrating, and is drawn back to his laptop. This happens without any great conscious awareness – he seems to be on autopilot.

Starting a task reduces our desire to procrastinate, but we may find ourselves becoming distracted if we feel frustrated, confused or anxious.

4 FINISHING THE TASK
Mike tries again and almost finishes the job. Then, just before the final dishes are loaded, he again becomes distracted. The dishwasher remains switched off, and Mike is procrastinating once more.

Many people struggle to finish tasks, becoming more stressed and anxious as the job nears completion.

5 THE TRANSITION FROM ONE TASK TO THE NEXT
Finally, Mike's dishwasher is fully loaded and switched on. He notices the kitchen surfaces need cleaning. Instead of making a start, he reaches for his laptop. He thinks: 'I'll do it in a minute.' With that thought, the procrastination process starts once more.

Making the transition from one task to the next can be difficult. The desire for 'a little rest' overwhelms our ability to keep going, and we procrastinate all over again.

Consider your own difficulties with procrastination – when do you most struggle?

Focus points

✻ *You are not a robot.* It is impossible to do everything perfectly.
✻ *Procrastination requires determination.* Wilfully delaying tasks is an act of determination, albeit a negative and destructive one.
✻ *Procrastination is a process.* Procrastination unfolds over several stages. Overcoming it involves changing the way we think, feel and behave at each stage.
✻ *Procrastination can strike at any time.* Whether starting a task, completing a task, or making the transition from one task to the next, knowing when you are at risk of procrastination helps you to overcome it.

Now that we have an idea of how procrastination works, let's look at how it can be changed.

How to use this book

Overcoming procrastination means *learning* to do things differently. The good news is: there is a solution – you can change. Many people will use the techniques in this book and accomplish much more with their lives. Let's explore how.

HOW DO WE CHANGE?

Personal change depends on acquiring new skills and remembering to use them:

▶ New skills are learned by repetition.

▶ There will be failure and success; both experiences count towards progress.

▶ With practice, these new skills become second nature – you can depend on them.

Learning requires effort. There will be some frustrating times ahead. You can mitigate this frustration by taking things at your own pace. Break things into small steps, and the challenges become manageable. For example, imagine learning and *applying* the following simple skills:

- the ability to recognize when you are procrastinating

- the ability to dismiss 'procrastination excuses'

- the ability to quickly break tasks down into simple steps

- the ability to ease past negative thoughts and feelings

- the ability to see the value of taking action

- the ability to motivate yourself so action take less effort

- the ability to build new, positive habits

- the ability to set goals and work towards the *important* matters in life.

Step by step, you will be taught these skills. They are not difficult to learn, but they do require thorough practice. Take things slowly and persevere – otherwise you will feel overwhelmed and give up. As you apply your new skills in day-to-day life, things will gradually improve.

LEARN ACTIVELY

You cannot learn the techniques in this book simply by reading about them – you have to put them into practice. No matter what the temptation, avoid glossing over the exercises. You will only change by *doing*. Learn actively. Use a notebook to write down your answers and thoughts.

EXPECT SOME FAILURE

Things will seem difficult at times. Anticipate this *pain barrier* – it means you are learning something. Regroup and try again. You will have gained some insight:

- You will fail, especially at first.

- When problems arise, ask yourself: 'What can I learn from this?'

- Learning comes from *trying* – give yourself time, and try again.

Understand *failure* and it becomes *feedback*. Resolve to keep going and your progress is virtually guaranteed.

KEEP AN OPEN MIND

Many techniques in this book will make sense, whereas others may seem pointless. Rather than dismissing exercises out of hand, test them first and keep an open mind. Our expectations are often confounded, and each exercise in this book has a purpose. Even if it doesn't seem logical at first, try it anyway. What have you got to lose?

SPEND TIME WITH POSITIVE PEOPLE

Do you know any positive, motivated people? If so, spend more time talking to them. Ask them how they are 'getting on'. Talk about the important things in life. Nothing motivates us more than other people's success – providing we set out to learn. Talk more to positive people and *your* success becomes more likely.

GET OUT OF YOUR COMFORT ZONE

Although procrastination can be debilitating, it is also *familiar*. Learning to do things differently takes you out of your comfort zone. For some, this will be too much; they will gloss over the exercises and eventually discard this book. You do not have to be one of those people – with practice, the unfamiliar becomes second nature.

Essential equipment

To begin – you will need a pen, a portable notepad (or electronic equivalent), and an open mind. You will be advised to write or print out information as you progress. A small noticeboard will be a good investment.

Quick fix: Assess an achievement

Think of something you can do well. It could be work, or a hobby, or being a parent. Remember learning these skills and focus on the details and use your notebook to write down your answers to the following questions:

* What did you learn?
* What challenges did you face?
* How did you overcome these challenges?

There is no right or wrong way to complete the exercise. Just remember a time when you pushed yourself out of your comfort zone. This *proves* you can do it.

Making a few significant changes can bring huge improvement. Overcoming procrastination is made easier by breaking things down into small steps. Learn skills thoroughly before racing ahead.

Focus points

✱ *Overcoming procrastination means doing things differently.* You cannot just think your way past procrastination – you have to try new things.

✱ *Learn actively: practise your new skills until you can depend on them.* Acquire simple skills and embed them before moving on. You will feel overwhelmed if you attempt too much at once.

✱ *You will hit the 'pain barrier' from time to time.* Expect some failure, and resolve to carry on. Persistence turns failure into an opportunity to learn. Keep going, and your progress is virtually guaranteed.

✱ *Keep an open mind.* Every exercise in this book has a purpose. Thoroughly engage with each technique, and you will learn something new – guaranteed!

Let's turn our attention to *your* procrastination. To begin changing it, you first need to identify what you procrastinate about.

Procrastination and you

When do you procrastinate? Do you only struggle with certain tasks, or do you procrastinate about everything – from the significant to the trivial? In either case we need to identify where procrastination holds you back.

Why did you buy this book? Has procrastination recently caused significant problems, or does life constantly sliding from your grasp? Let's get a clearer picture.

EXERCISE: PROCRASTINATION CHECKLIST

▶ This simple exercise takes one minute.

▶ The aim is to get a clear picture of your procrastination.

Read through this checklist and tick the relevant boxes or copy it into your notebook. If other causes of procrastination occur to you, make a note of those in the relevant section, too.

Work:
- ❏ Returning or making phone calls
- ❏ Meeting deadlines
- ❏ Starting or finishing projects
- ❏ Routine tasks
- ❏ Answering emails or post
- ❏ Starting difficult tasks
- ❏ Applying for new jobs
- ❏ Learning new skills
- ❏ Changing career

Study or self-development:
- ❏ Enrolling at college or university
- ❏ Attending lectures
- ❏ Studying for exams
- ❏ Starting essays or assignments
- ❏ Attending group classes
- ❏ Learning a new skill
- ❏ Writing academic papers
- ❏ Working on a book or Ph.D.
- ❏ Starting a new hobby or pastime

Health:
- ❏ Starting a diet
- ❏ Starting an exercise programme
- ❏ Stopping smoking or drinking
- ❏ Making medical appointments
- ❏ Attending medical appointments
- ❏ Responding to health difficulties
- ❏ Personal hygiene (showering, teeth, etc.)
- ❏ Learning to meditate
- ❏ Learning to overcome procrastination

Social:
- ❏ Making or returning phone calls
- ❏ Starting or ending a relationship
- ❏ Being assertive
- ❏ Being affectionate or communicative
- ❏ Attending or arranging social events
- ❏ Discussing problems
- ❏ Replying to invitations
- ❏ Going to the cinema
- ❏ Contacting friends

Household chores:
- ❑ Daily chores (tidying, cooking, etc.)
- ❑ Larger chores (cleaning, ironing, etc.)
- ❑ Getting ready for work
- ❑ Spring-cleaning the house
- ❑ Maintenance and repairs
- ❑ Food shopping
- ❑ Gardening
- ❑ Running errands

Personal:
- ❑ Opening mail
- ❑ Paying bills
- ❑ Budgeting finances
- ❑ Tax returns and other financial tasks
- ❑ Making plans for the future
- ❑ Carrying out plans when the time is right
- ❑ Making decisions
- ❑ Committing to change or new challenges
- ❑ Learning to drive

Is there a discernible pattern? Do you procrastinate in just one area of your life, or do you struggle across the board? While working through this book, update this checklist if new areas come to light. You will benefit by being comprehensive.

Moving on

Everybody procrastinates from time to time; we are not perfect, and our lives reflect this fact. Even the most positive people will have moments where they *just cannot be bothered*.

However – serious procrastination can ruin lives. It is a problem worth tackling. You will have to learn new skills and overcome challenges, but positive change can happen.

▶ Procrastination is a process. Whenever you find yourself procrastinating, identify the various stages as they happen.

▶ Procrastination is not the same as 'being lazy'. It has many causes and reflects a complex interplay of thought, emotion, belief and behaviour. Avoid labelling yourself.

▶ Personal change means learning new skills in the right order.

▶ This book will introduce you to many new techniques. They are not difficult to master when taken at a steady pace. Accomplish this and you will progress.

▶ As you work through this book, update the checklist (above) whenever necessary. Build a comprehensive picture of your procrastination, and you'll know precisely what needs to change.

Next step

To learn new skills, you need something to focus on. In the next chapter we will set a 'practice goal'. This will give you a reason to engage with the exercises, and the desire to make progress.

2

Setting goals

In this chapter you will learn:

▶ *How to define clear goals using the SMART technique*

▶ *How to set up an experimental practice goal for the purposes of this book and to construct a goal worksheet to help you to decide on the outcomes you are looking to reach*

▶ *How to break down your goal into small, manageable steps*

▶ *The importance of recognizing that time is a precious commodity and that your actions now really do help to create your future.*

? How do you feel?

1 Do you know what your goals are in life?

2 Do you wish you had more focus?

3 Do you often feel overwhelmed?

4 Do you want to be more organized?

5 Do you want to know what to do next?

It is easy to get lost without a map; it's the difference between driving around aimlessly and arriving at your destination.

In the previous chapter you identified when you tend to procrastinate. A major cause of procrastination is *not knowing where to start*. To remedy this you need a clear goal. Even if you have read about goal-setting elsewhere, read on. The exercises in this chapter are essential to the rest of this book.

A goal is simply an *end result*. It can be large or small, simple or complex. Goals give us focus; they help us plan and measure our progress. Without clear goals you *will* drift – this much is guaranteed.

Mythbuster: 'I don't need to write my goals down'

Some people believe writing their goals down is pointless. Instead, their goals *remain in their heads*. They think: 'What difference does it make? Anyway, I haven't got the time!'

But it does make a difference. Well-defined goals are too detailed to keep track of mentally. Goals improve our focus, but only when they are clear. When are kept solely in our minds, they are fuzzy, ill-defined and easy to forget.

Write goals down and they become tangible. This fosters belief and makes it harder to come up with excuses. Perhaps this is why people feel reluctant. If you have no time to write down your goals, how will you find the time to achieve them?

Setting the right goal

Goal-setting is not complicated. Follow a few simple steps, and everything becomes clear. To begin we will set just one 'practice goal'. Sticking to one goal is vital. It is impossible to change everything at once, you would just become overwhelmed. There will be more goals in future – for now, have just a little patience.

Turn to the checklist in Chapter 1 or the copy in your notebook. Which boxes did you tick? Where is procrastination a problem? If you could address just one thing, what would it be?

▶ Do you have an approaching deadline?

▶ Does an area of your life urgently need 'sorting'?

▶ Would achieving something now significantly improve your life?

It makes sense to practise the techniques in this book *and* improve your life at the same time. Your practice goal should achieve both, and ideally match these criteria:

▶ Choose a goal that involves a significant amount of work, including simple and complex tasks.

▶ Choose a goal you can work towards daily (or near-daily). One task per month is no use; select a goal that requires frequent attention, and which you could complete within a month or two.

▶ If possible, ease yourself into this process. Avoid starting with a critical goal unless you have a pressing need.

▶ To begin, choose an 'approach' goal, e.g. *starting an exercise programme*, rather than an 'avoidance' goal, e.g. *quitting smoking*. You can focus on 'avoidance' goals later.

Do your potential goals meet these criteria? Here are some ideas:

▶ Getting a big project out of the way

▶ Starting an exercise routine

▶ De-cluttering your home and completing DIY projects

▶ Sorting out your financial affairs

- Completing a study programme
- Mastering a new sport or hobby
- Finding a new job.

And so on...

After completing your first goal, you can always define a second – and then a third. Take a moment now to identify (up to) four *potential* goals you could work towards. Describe each goal in just one sentence, writing them down in your notebook.

How many potential goals did you come up with? Next, let's narrow your choice down to just one.

Defining clear goals

What constitutes a well-defined goal? Perhaps you have read about SMART goals previously:

- **Specific tasks:** what tasks do you need to complete to achieve your goal? Who else is involved? Where will the goal be achieved?

- **Measurable outcomes:** how will you know when you have achieved your goal? What will be different? What will you have gained or taken care of? What problems will you have resolved? What milestones will you have reached?

- **Attainable:** your goal should stretch you – otherwise you'll soon feel bored. It should also be realistic, or you will quickly feel discouraged.

- **Relevant:** your goal should be meaningful – otherwise why bother? You could address long-standing problems, or achieve a long-held desire. A relevant goal reflects the narrative of your life.

- **Time-based:** a goal is a dream with a *deadline*. How long will it take to achieve your goal?

Define your goals with these factors in mind and you are much more likely to achieve them. Let's look at each point in more detail.

SPECIFIC TASKS

Defining the action required to achieve your goal is vital. You need to know where to start, what to do next, and how to progress from there. For example:

▶ *I am going to lose weight and get fitter:*

> ▷ I will cut out all bread, dairy and sugary foods.

> ▷ I will eat salads and protein.

> ▷ I will do cardio and weights in the gym five days per week.

> ▷ I will drink a minimum of two litres of water per day.

▶ *I am going to write my dissertation:*

> ▷ I will write a list of books I need to buy.

> ▷ I will go through each book and make brief notes.

> ▷ I will devise a comprehensive list of chapters for my dissertation.

> ▷ I will expand that list by adding the topics for each chapter.

> ▷ I will start writing Chapter 3 – I have the most experience in that area.

Look through your four potential goals. Briefly estimate the action involved with each one. To get the most from this book, an effective *practice goal* should involve a significant number of tasks.

MEASURABLE OUTCOMES

How will you will know when you have achieved your goal? Sometimes, the outcomes match the specific tasks defined earlier. For example:

▶ *I will know I am losing weight because:*

> ▷ The scales do not lie! I will be 14 pounds lighter

> ▷ I will be regularly eating salads and protein, with no grains, sugars and dairy

> ▷ I will be going to the gym five days per week

> ▷ I will be drinking two litres of water per day.

▶ *I will know when I have thoroughly prepared to write my dissertation because:*

▷ I will have all of the books I need

▷ I will have made notes on all of these books

▷ I will have a list of chapters I want to write

▷ This list of chapters will include the relevant topics I want to explore

▷ I will be ready to make a start on Chapter 3.

As you can see, there is some duplication here. If your specific task is to 'clean the kitchen sink', it may seem pointless to define the measurable outcome as: 'I will have a clean kitchen sink!' However, knowing precisely what to expect brings accountability, focus and motivation. Measurable outcomes prevent cheating. Knowing the sink *has to be clean* means you cannot pretend otherwise.

Knowing your desired outcomes connects you to your goal, enhancing your appreciation of the rewards involved and boosting motivation. Even if seemingly redundant, this thoroughness eventually pays off.

ATTAINABLE
Setting impossible goals will get you nowhere. For our practice goal, be realistic and set something achievable.

In future, when procrastination is a thing of the past, set the bar high and aim for the important things in life. *Improbable* goals are still achievable, but allow yourself time to build up to them.

RELEVANT
Your practice goal should teach you how to overcome procrastination *and* improve your life. If you are an efficient machine at work, but struggle to keep a tidy home life ... set a goal relating to your home life! Setting a goal that teaches you nothing is pointless.

TIME-BASED

Defining a time limit for your goal is important, otherwise you will lose focus, become complacent, and continue to struggle with procrastination. Identify a realistic timeframe for your goal: too tight, or too distant, and it becomes meaningless.

People who procrastinate often struggle with time. Learning to appreciate time represents a step in the right direction.

Focus points

* *A goal is an end result.* Goals help us plan and measure our progress.
* *Goals should be SMART.* A well-defined goal includes specific tasks and measurable outcomes. It is attainable, relevant and time-based.
* *Use this chapter to set a 'practice goal'.* Your practice goal should help you to experiment with the exercises in this book *and* improve your life. Set a goal you can work towards on a daily (or near-daily) basis.

Well-formed goals involve a lot of detail – too much to carry solely in our minds. This is why goals should be written down; they become real and tangible. To see how goal-setting works in real life, let's review another case study.

Case study: Maya's story

Maya is a keen amateur photographer. She recently enrolled on an expensive photography course, but is procrastinating about starting it. Maya finds this difficult to understand because she is passionate about photography.

Maya decided to set a well-formed goal. Figure 2.1 shows her answers to the goal worksheet she came up with.

Let's review Maya's progress so far:

▶ She has stated her goal clearly.

▶ She knows the outcomes she hopes to achieve.

▶ She has explained why the goal is important, and how it will benefit her.

▶ She has set a realistic deadline.

GOAL WORKSHEET

What is your goal (stated in positive terms)?

I am going to complete the photography correspondence course I signed up to last year.

Measurable outcomes: How will you know when you have reached the goal?

▶ What will you see or hear when you have achieved your goal?
▶ What quantity or numbers can you put on the outcome?
▶ What specific bad feelings will go away?
▶ What good feelings will you feel?

I will have read all of the course modules, and taken the required photographs.

I will have submitted my photography to the course tutor and received feedback.

I will have completed the 100 hours' study time recommended by the course materials.

I will have revised for and completed the course exam.

Relevant: How is this goal significant to you?

▶ Why is it important to you?
▶ *What would it mean if you didn't achieve the goal?*
▶ What would it mean if you did achieve the goal?

Completing this course is really important to me because I love photography and I want to improve my ability.

I spent a lot of money on this course. I don't want my photography stagnate.

It would mean so much to finish the course and improve my photography because I spend so much time practising it.

Time-based:

▶ When will you reach this goal?
▶ What time limit can you put on this goal?
▶ How long do you need to work at your goal for?

If I can spend ten hours per week on the course (one day at weekend, and a couple of hours during the week), I can have it complete within ten weeks. Let's say 12 weeks to be safe - so in three months' time from today.

Figure 2.1 Maya's goal worksheet

Next, Maya 'brainstormed' a list of tasks required to achieve her goal. Here is how she did it.

Maya read through the four measurable outcomes associated with her goal:

1 *I will have read all of the course modules, and taken the required photographs.*

2 *I will have submitted my photography to the course tutor and received feedback.*

3 *I will have completed the 100 hours' study time recommended by the course materials.*

4 *I will have revised for and completed the course exam.*

Using a blank piece of A4 paper, she wrote her goal in the middle of the page – like so:

PASS MY PHOTOGRAPHY COURSE

She then closed her eyes and pictured those desired outcomes in her mind: reading course materials, taking photographs, receiving feedback, revising for the exam, etc. Maya then wondered: 'How can I make this possible? What do I need to do?' As answers popped into her mind, she scribbled them onto the sheet of paper.

After five minutes or so, her sheet of paper looked like this:

Set aside some time during the week by cancelling the book club

Make Sundays my 'photography day'

Buy a pen and notepad to make notes

Install some new photo-editing software

Clear some desk space to study

Upgrade the camera software

PASS MY PHOTOGRAPHY COURSE

Understand each course module

List the types of photos I need to take for each module

Speak to Graham at the photography club about the course

Email the course tutor and introduce myself, and ask her about the exam

Buy the 'recommended reading' books and subscribe to the suggested newsletters

Phone Lizzie and the others, see if they are interested in taking photos on Sundays

---

Even at this early stage, Maya's list is quite comprehensive. Some tasks are very simple: e.g. introducing herself to the course tutor. Others will require repeated action – for instance, studying the course materials. Gathered together, these ideas form the basis of her '*action* plan'.

Maya rewrote her ideas into a list, fleshing out the bare bones with more detail. Where tasks seemed too big to accomplish all in one go, or if they seemed vague, she broke them down further. Here is her list:

- Set aside some time during the week (Tuesdays) by cancelling the book club.
  - ▷ Call Rebecca and leave the book club.
  - ▷ Set a reminder on my phone to leave on time on Tuesdays.
- Clear some desk space to study.
  - ▷ Sort through the papers on the desk: throw away the old ones, file the new ones.
  - ▷ Clean the computer screen.
- Buy equipment (via the Internet?).
  - ▷ Buy a new, comfier chair.
  - ▷ Buy a pen and notepad.
  - ▷ Buy some box files (for the desk papers).
  - ▷ Buy some photo-editing software, and download the free camera software.
  - ▷ Buy the recommended books.
  - ▷ Subscribe to the suggested photography newsletters.
- Install the new photo-editing software.
- Install the new camera software.
- Speak to Graham at the photography club about the course.
- Email the course tutor and introduce myself, and ask her about the exam.
- Understand each course module.
- List the types of photos I need to take for each module.
- Phone Lizzie and the others to see if they are interested in taking photos on Sundays.
- Make Sundays my 'photography day'.

This list describes everything that needs to be done. Large, vague tasks are now more detailed, and each task is written using action-oriented language. For example, 'find out about course' lacks direction, whereas 'speak to Graham at the photography club about the course' is more helpful. Using specific language to describe action enhances our focus and clarity.

Quick fix: Allocate more time than necessary

Deciding how long tasks take is tricky. As a general rule, allocate more time than necessary. Things will inevitably go wrong at some stage.

The same principle applies to your goals. If you think it will take a month, allocate two! As you learn to motivate yourself, this spare time becomes yours to enjoy. If things do go wrong, you still have time to deal with the consequences.

Maya then revised the list a final time, re-ordering the tasks into a sequential, time-based order. Some tasks were not time-sensitive, so she started with those. She then identified those tasks that *had* to come first, and continued from there. Her list now looked like this:

Complete first:

▶ Set aside some time during the week (Tuesdays) by cancelling the book club.

    ▷ Call Rebecca and leave the book club.

    ▷ Set a remember on my phone to leave on time on Tuesdays.

▶ Email the course tutor and introduce myself, and ask her about the exam.

▶ Speak to Graham at the photography club about the course.

▶ Phone Lizzie and the others to see if they are interested in taking photos on Sundays.

▶ Buy equipment (via the Internet?).

    ▷ Buy a new, comfier chair.

    ▷ Buy a pen and notepad.

- ▷ Buy some box files (for the desk papers).
- ▷ Buy some photo-editing software, and download the free camera software.
- ► Buy the recommended books.
- ► Subscribe to the suggested photography newsletters.

When the equipment arrives:

- ► Clear some desk space to study.
- ► Sort through the papers on the desk: throw away the old ones, file the new ones.
- ► Clean the computer screen.
- ► Install the new photo-editing software.
- ► Install the new camera software.

When I have the working space sorted (Sunday):

- ► Understand each course module.
- ► List the types of photos I need to take for each module.
- ► Make Sundays my 'photography day'.

Maya now has a comprehensive action plan. She knows exactly what to do and when. She will achieve her goal by accomplishing these steps.

At this point, Maya was making excellent progress: calling people, sending emails and buying equipment for her workspace. She de-cluttered her desk with no problem, and installed the new software onto her computer. In fact, she only started to procrastinate when she arrived at the task 'Make notes about each course module'. Then, everything ground to a halt.

Maya felt dismayed to find herself procrastinating, particularly after her initial success. With some reflection she identified the problem: *the task was too big, too vague.* She did not know where to start. She overcame this by revising her plan further, breaking the task down into smaller steps:

▷ Understand each course module.

   ▷ Read through the module, making brief notes.

   ▷ Turn those notes into 'mind maps'.

   ▷ Test myself about each module, by reading about it on the Internet and gauging how much I understand.

Being specific about *what needed to be done* helped Maya tremendously, and she resumed her good progress. Whenever you procrastinate you should ask: 'Do I know what to do next?' A clear list of simple tasks changes everything.

> **Focus points**
>
> ✱ *Set comprehensive goals.* State realistic goals clearly, know the outcomes, know why they are important, and set deadlines.
> ✱ *Break your goals into individual tasks.* Consider the outcomes you hope you achieve, and ask yourself: 'What do I need to do to make this happen?' Write down every idea, no matter how small or obvious.
> ✱ *Compile your ideas into a list.* Where tasks seem too big or vague, break them into smaller steps. Fill in the gaps.
> ✱ *Then, order your list chronologically.* Start with the tasks that need to come first, and take it from there.

Later in this chapter you will devise your own action plan, but first let's examine a question rarely raised in self-help books...

Why do anything?

Life is all too brief, and tinged with sadness and pain. In this context, procrastination seems so fruitless. The constant delays create great heartache. It is stressful and deeply unrewarding.

Our goals needn't be grandiose, just important to us. Lives are enriched by achievement; it staves off the pain of regret in old age. By contrast, procrastination leads to missed opportunities. And nothing causes greater sadness.

So here is the point: improve your life and it *actually* feels better. Obvious, perhaps, but difficult to see when procrastination takes hold. Logic is lost to irrationality and fear, and opportunities pass us by. Life is difficult enough, even without procrastination.

The answer to the question 'Why do anything?' is simple. Do nothing, and it will eventually *hurt*. Hopefully this makes sense to you. If it does, we have work to do.

Setting your practice goal

This book will help with day-to-day procrastination, but learning the techniques will be easier if, initially, you focus on a single practice goal. When setting future goals, follow this same process.

EXERCISE: SETTING A GOAL

> ▶ This exercise takes 5–10 minutes.
>
> ▶ The aim is to identify a practice goal you can work towards on a daily basis.
>
> ▶ Use this exercise to set goals.

1 Previously, you listed four potential goals you could work towards. Review that list now:

   ▷ Will these potential goals stretch you?

   ▷ Are they important to you?

   ▷ Can you work on them daily (or near-daily)?

2 If not, you can always come up with a new goal. Before making a final decision, consider these points:

   ▷ Choose an 'approach goal', stated in positive, concrete terms: 'Exercise daily until my weight drops to 170 pounds', rather than 'Lose some weight'.

   ▷ Identify the measurable outcomes associated with your goal. What will you see, hear or feel when you have achieved your goal? What milestones will you need to reach? What will you gain, or what will be different? Reread Maya's example if you are uncertain.

   ▷ How is this goal relevant to your life? Are you passionate about it? How will you be rewarded? What's in it for you? Aim to improve your life but remember – you will be practising new skills. Don't set something *too* challenging initially.

> ▷ How long will it take to achieve your goal? When can you finish by?

3 Next, copy and fill out the worksheet shown in Figure 2.2. Do not skip this step! Getting your goals down on paper is vital. Take your time – there is no rush.

When you look at your goal, how does it make you feel? Excited? Stressed? Anxious? Sceptical? Either way, engage with the next exercise fully. You will improve your positivity and belief in future chapters. For now, let's define the steps you need to take.

EXERCISE: LISTING EVERY STEP

▶ This exercise takes 10–5 minutes.

▶ The aim is to identify the steps required to achieve your goal.

▶ Use this exercise whenever you set a goal.

1 To begin, write your confidence goal (in full) in the middle of a blank sheet of A4 paper.

2 Reread the measurable outcomes associated with your goal. Close your eyes and imagine experiencing them. Then ask yourself: 'What do I need to do to make this happen?' Scribble down whatever task you can think of; anything that will contribute – directly or indirectly, big or small – towards your goal. Think about:

> ▷ **Simple tasks.** Achieving goals means ticking boxes. What tasks do you need to complete?

> ▷ **Habits.** Some goals require repetitious action – what habits do you need to build? What bad habits do you need to stop?

> ▷ **Skills.** What skills do you need to achieve your goal? How could you develop those skills?

GOAL WORKSHEET

What is your goal (stated in positive terms)?

_____

▶ _____

Measurable outcomes: How will you know when you have reached the goal?

▶ What will you see or hear when you have achieved your goal?

▶ What quantity or numbers can you put on the outcome?

▶ What specific bad feelings will go away? What good feelings will you feel?

_____

_____

_____

_____

_____

_____

Relevant: How is this goal significant to you?

▶ Why is it important to you?

▶ What would it mean if you didn't achieve the goal?

▶ What would it mean if you did achieve the goal?

_____

_____

_____

_____

Time-based: When will you reach this goal?

▶ What time limit can you put on this goal?

▶ How long do you need to work at your goal for?

_____

_____

_____

_____

Figure 2.2 Goal worksheet

3 Let your pen run free and scribble ideas down quickly. Don't censor your thoughts or put them in any order – you will sort through them later. Be as comprehensive as possible – write everything down, no matter how small or obvious.

Spend a good 10–15 minutes on this, and write down every possible task. When finished, take a 20-minute break.

* * * * *

1 Welcome back. Next, review your list of ideas. Are there any glaring omissions? When you are happy with your list, move on to the next step.

2 Ask yourself: 'What do I need to do first? And then what? And then what?' Where should you start? How do you progress from there?

3 Then, write out these tasks in a list format (ideally using a computer). Start with the first actions you'll need to complete, and progress from there.

4 Finally, ensure they are in a sequential, time-based order. If required, break large or vague tasks into smaller chunks. If you get stuck, review Maya's example from earlier in this chapter.

How many tasks are on your list? Did you break them down into smaller steps? Does the order seem about right? Remember, you can review this plan as we go along – nothing is set in stone.

Defining clear goals is not easy. By doing so, you have taken a huge step in the right direction. This already sets you apart. You should take a moment to feel proud – this achievement is not to be underestimated.

And – if you have yet to complete the goal-setting exercise, it is not too late. Consider starting now. The next exercise will help.

Why bother now?

As life flows by, moment to moment, we cannot keep track of *everything*. But everything counts towards something, no matter how big or small. Whether you pursue your goals or procrastinate, your life's story will ultimately reflect your decision.

Have you completed the exercises in this chapter? Either way, let's look at consequences in more detail.

EXERCISE: UNDERSTANDING THE CONSEQUENCES

▶ This exercise takes 5–10 minutes.

▶ The aim of this exercise is to fully comprehend the cause of our actions.

▶ Use this exercise whenever you set goals.

1 Think about *not* achieving your goal. What are the consequences? Bear the following questions in mind and write your answers in your notebook:

   ▷ If I avoid this goal, I will stay in my comfort zone. Will I gain anything else?

   ▷ If I avoid this goal, how will I miss out? What is the cost? What will I lose?

   ▷ What will change – for better or worse – if I avoid this goal?

2 Then, think about achieving your goal. Again – what are the consequences? Answer the following questions, and again write your answers beneath the other ones in your notebook:

   ▷ What will I gain by achieving this goal?

   ▷ Will achieving this goal mean I lose something?

   ▷ What will it cost me to achieve this goal?

   ▷ What will be different, better, or worse?

Reflect on your answers for a moment. Is it in your *best interests* to achieve this goal? If so, do you want to start now, or would you prefer to delay further? Procrastination is a question of *timing*, so let's look at how much time you have to spend.

EXERCISE: HOW MUCH TIME DO YOU REALLY HAVE?

▶ This exercise takes five minutes.

▶ The aim of this exercise is to demonstrate how limited our time really is.

1 Draw a large circle on a blank sheet of paper. Divide it into half, then quarters, and then eighths.

2 Imagine each segment represents a decade in your life. How much time has passed so far? If you're 40, shade in 4 segments, if you're 27, shade in 2.7 segments, and so on... This is your time elapsed already.

3 We spend a third of our lives asleep, so shade in *one-third* of the remaining segments.

4 How many segments remain? Next, shade in half of what is left. On average, we spend 40 years of our lives working, studying, carrying out domestic chores, spending time with the kids, commuting, and watching TV. This time is *taken*.

5 Now – take a long look. How much time do you have left? Do you *actually* have time to waste?

This exercise may leave you feeling anxious or even miserable. It can be shocking to realize how quickly our time is spent. Time sweeps all of us out to sea, eventually... The question is: Do you swim against the tide, or do you give up and wait to drown?

Quick fix: Your actions count

Imagine yourself, five years from now, taking a moment to reflect. Life is good, you feel satisfied with your achievements, and you're ready for more.

This moment in time could exist; it depends on your actions *today*. Everything we do counts towards some future version of ourselves.

Whether five years from now, or six months from now, it helps to cast your mind forward and connect with your future. Remember – your actions *today* have consequences. This cannot be denied.

A time to act

How much has your procrastination cost you? Do you even know what you are waiting for? Time is your most precious resource. You are reading this book, so complete what you have started. You are the only person who can act on your intentions.

So – *right now* – do one of the following:

▶ Type up your goal (include all of the sections: the outcomes, the relevance, the deadlines, etc.), and your action plan. Then print it out and pin it to the wall, ideally where you will see it each day.

▶ Or, if you have still not completed the goal-setting exercise in this chapter – start it now.

Given the subject matter of this book, you may *still* feel tempted to skip this step. Understand – this one simple act will change everything. Visible goals are achievable, whereas goals hidden from view mostly go unfulfilled.

If you're still resisting, review the time you have left and think: '*OK – I'll just do this one thing...*' Muster everything you have to start. In time, old stress and misery will be transformed. And you will be free.

Moving on

The *practice goal* you have set today will be referred to throughout this book. You also have an *action plan* – tasks to focus on while practising new skills, and which will help you achieve your goal.

Many people find clear goals significantly decrease procrastination. They are a great place to start. Before moving on to the next chapter, reread your goal and your action plan. Make sure you're happy with your choices, and remember – you can revise it as we make progress.

▶ Having a goal creates a positive mindset. As you know what to aim for, you can plan and measure your progress. Without goals, you are bound to drift through life.

▶ Well-formed goals include *specific tasks* and *measurable outcomes*, and are *attainable*, *relevant* and *time-based*.

▶ Break goals down into specific tasks, and they become easier to achieve. Use action-oriented language, order each task chronologically, and simplify large or vague tasks even further. Do this and you have your *action plan*.

▶ No matter how much time you *think* you have left, it is still your most precious resource. Whenever you procrastinate, remember how valuable time is. This will prepare you for the exercises to come.

→ Next step

In the next chapter, we will look at *activating situations* – those key moments when procrastination strikes. Learn to spot the warning signs, and procrastination becomes easier to manage.

Building awareness

In this chapter you will learn:

▶ *The importance of raising your awareness of your own procrastination thoughts and behaviours and of analysing the situations where these arise*

▶ *To use the 'ABC model' to provide insights into the 'activating situations' – the specific circumstances – that give rise to your procrastination*

▶ *That a thorough understanding of your own specific 'activating situations' is a vital first step towards mastering procrastination and moving forward in this book.*

? How do you feel?

1 Do you bury your head in the sand?

2 Do you wonder where the time goes?

3 Do you find yourself procrastinating without realizing it?

4 Are you always late?

5 Do you sometimes wonder how you got yourself into 'this mess'?

Procrastination is the thief of time... Work piles up, promises are broken, and we bury our head in the sand. Procrastination can also be subtle, and we barely notice as hours fly by. In this chapter, you will learn to recognize procrastination in its various guises.

The multifaceted mind

Being human is a complicated matter...

Right now, your brain is performing sophisticated tasks – for example, processing information, controlling your movement, accessing and storing memories, and orchestrating your comprehension of language (to name just a few). As a result, you *experience being you* – it is a reality you can understand.

As you read these words, you might be aware of 'your voice' in your mind. You might be aware of your environment, your comfort level, or of the time of day. But you will *not* be aware of your brain's activity. The experience of 'being you' depends on processes that take place beyond your conscious awareness. And some of these processes are designed to *override* your control.

In the same vein, we are not consciously aware of our whole mind. There are beliefs, values, hopes and fears woven through the fabric of your being. People are complex and contradictory, and procrastination reflects this. It is a facet of our humanity.

Knowing your own mind

To remedy procrastination we must tease through the detail of your thoughts and emotions; resolving bottlenecks, transcending limitations and changing perspectives. You will need new skills to accomplish this.

When we struggle with procrastination, our minds are not wholly integrated. We procrastinate because *a part of us* believes it makes sense to delay. This is not a rational part of us; rather, our logic is overridden. We then experience internal conflict and turmoil. *Procrastination is being in two minds at once.*

To change procrastination, you need to learn how that happens.

Focus points

✳ *Your brain is complex.* Even now, it is making countless calculations. Your experience of 'being you' depends on this.

✳ *Our awareness is limited.* Most of your brain's activity is unconscious, but some of this activity is powerful – it overrides your conscious control.

✳ *We are not simple, single-minded creatures.* Our minds are nuanced and multifaceted, and sometimes subject to internal turmoil.

✳ *Overcoming procrastination starts with becoming more self-aware.* When we procrastinate, it is because we are in two minds. To begin, we need to learn how that happens.

Thoughts, feelings and behaviours

Our minds are complex, but emotions and behaviours *also* play a part in procrastination, complicating matters further. It affects us in different ways and on different levels.

Do you recognize *thoughts* such as:

▶ 'I'll do this later, when I have everything I need.'

▶ 'I don't know where to begin – I should leave it for now.'

▶ 'It's OK to just watch the rest of this TV programme; *then* I'll make a start.'

Procrastination leads to certain *emotions*:

▶ anxious or resistant feelings in your chest or stomach

▶ a kind of *braced resistance* when you think about taking action

▶ a sense of temptation to do something else instead.

Our *behaviour* changes when we procrastinate – for example:

▶ We avoid tasks by focusing on less important matters.

▶ We take little breaks while switching from one task to the next.

▶ We dither endlessly, unable to sit down and make a start.

Our thoughts, emotions, and behaviours interact constantly as we move from moment to moment. *This is our state of being*, and it explains why procrastination overwhelms us. For example:

▶ **Thoughts change emotions and behaviours:** Think about procrastinating, and you may *feel temptation*. Procrastination then becomes more likely. Your thoughts have changed your feelings and behaviour.

▶ **Emotions change thoughts and behaviours:** Feel hesitant about taking action, and you may *excuse* yourself from taking action. Again, procrastination becomes likely. Your feelings have modified your thoughts and behaviour.

▶ **Behaviours change thoughts and feelings:** When you procrastinate, your thoughts and feelings become even more focused on *avoidance*. In this example, your behaviour has directed your thoughts and emotions.

Surprisingly, even though procrastination changes so much, recognizing it can prove difficult. There are an infinite number of ways to procrastinate, and sometimes we barely notice.

Mythbuster: People are always aware of what they're doing

The average person breathes around 12 times per minute, or around 18,000–20,000 times per day. How many of these breaths have you been aware of today?

We think even more than we breathe. On average, a person thinks up to 50,000 thoughts in one day. How many thoughts can you remember? Could you list the thoughts you've had in the past hour?

We are only dimly aware of our thoughts; they just *pop* into our minds and fall into the past. There is more to *being you* than you know. Give up the illusion of perfect awareness — it does not exist.

Changing procrastination begins by building greater awareness. Learning to recognize the warning signs is a good place to start.

Awareness of procrastination

There are generally three types of procrastination: *denial*, *refusal* and *delay*:

1 **Denial:** In low-stress situations, we ignore our commitments and focus elsewhere; for example, if you have an exam three months from now, you can forget about it. This style of procrastination involves *little* or *no* awareness.

2 **Refusal:** Quickly rejecting action and focusing elsewhere is known as refusal. This style of procrastination involves only *fleeting* awareness. We quickly move on, having succeeded in our aim to avoid. This style of procrastination includes putting things off until tomorrow.

3 **Delay:** Generally, stress increases awareness. Important tasks, which cannot be *denied* or *refused*, cause us to *delay*.

We may 'perfectly' plan tasks instead of just getting on with them. Or we might repeatedly succumb to distraction: Facebook, Twitter, phone calls, less important tasks, endless cups of tea...

When faced with important tasks, procrastination becomes stressful and upsetting. We feel bemused and frustrated, anxious or guilty. It would be sensible to *just make a start*, but logic doesn't come into it. At this point, we are stuck.

These categories are not mutually exclusive; procrastination is best described by the *process you go through and point you arrive at*:

▶ If you mostly ignore tasks, this is *denial*.

▶ If you think about tasks fleetingly before rejecting them, this is *refusal*.

▶ If you cannot put tasks out of your mind, but make no significant progress, this is *delay*.

These are generalizations, of course. Procrastination is a facet of consciousness, and just as fluid. It grows strong within our nature, and then falls away. Procrastination is personal to you.

Quick fix: Cultivate greater awareness

Cultivating greater awareness is straightforward and worthwhile. Practise, and you'll develop greater control over your thoughts, feelings and behaviour.

Learning any skill can be frustrating at first, but persevere with these two simple exercises and you will benefit.

Awareness exercise 1

For the next 60 seconds, focus *only* on your breathing. So:
1 Set a timer on your phone.
2 Focus your awareness only your breathing.
3 Keep your eyes open and breathe normally.
4 Whenever your mind wanders (and it will) bring your full awareness back to your breathing.
It sounds simple, but, to begin with, your mind *will* wander.

Awareness exercise 2

When you have mastered the first exercise, try this for the next 60 seconds:
1 Sit, comfortably, and focus on your breathing.
2 Then, using the phrase 'right now...' describe everything you become aware of – e.g. 'Right now, I can see the wall in front of me...', 'Right now, I can hear a dog barking outside,' and so on...
3 Use your senses: comment on what you can see, feel, hear, taste and smell.
4 Whenever your mind wanders (to the past, or the future, or wherever), bring it back to the present moment and simply observe.

These exercises are trickier than they sound, but they will strengthen your awareness of procrastination. Ideally, practise three or four times per day. They take only a minute to complete.

Do you often procrastinate without realizing it? If *low awareness* is a feature of your procrastination, resolve to pay more attention from this point. These two awareness exercises will help, particularly when you know how it *feels* to procrastinate.

Recognizing procrastination

A simple way to identify procrastination is to ask yourself a few questions:

▶ 'Am I in denial about an important task?'*

▶ 'Have I just rejected the idea of doing something?'

▶ 'Am I just delaying here?'

▶ 'What am I actually doing?'

*Note: There is always something we are *supposed* to be doing! Use common sense, and ask this question only about the pressing tasks.

Check in with yourself periodically; ask yourself these questions and become more aware of your thoughts, your feelings and your actions.

There is another way to identify procrastination – by understanding how it *feels*.

EXERCISE: HOW DOES IT FEEL TO PROCRASTINATE?

▶ This exercise takes five minutes.

▶ The aim is to identify a task that will cause you to procrastinate.

1 In the previous chapter you devised an *action plan*. Read through it now, and select a task you could start today. Write the task in your notebook – thus:

A task or job I could do right now:

_____

_____

_____

2 Next, focus on the task and ask yourself: 'Why is it in my best interests to do this task? How will it benefit me?' Write a brief answer. For example:

▷ 'Cleaning and tidying the house means I'll enjoy my living environment more.'

▷ 'It's good to contact my friends – they'll know what I'm up to and I'll feel more connected to people.'

▷ 'A good physical workout now would be good for my health.'

▷ 'Rehanging that door will stop everyone getting frustrated with it... including me!'

It is in my best interests to start this job now because:

_____

_____

_____

Having confirmed the task as being in your best interests, now ask yourself: 'Is it in my best interests to start this now?' Irrational excuses don't count – be honest with yourself. What is your answer?

3 Next, focus on the task and think about starting it. If you were asked to put this book down and begin the task immediately – what would your response be? Think seriously about the answer.

You know it is in your best interests to start this task *now*. Unless you want to start immediately (and some readers might), *you are now in touch with the very essence of procrastination – the desire to avoid.*

4 What type of procrastination was it?

▷ Unable to complete the exercise because you haven't set a goal? This is *denial*.

▷ Read through the exercise without engaging with it? This is *denial*.

▷ Read through the exercise, but quickly rejected the idea of taking action? This is *refusal*.

▷ Completed the exercise, but felt reluctant to start the task? This is *delay*.

5 How did it feel to procrastinate?

▷ Perhaps you felt an emotion – a jab of pain or fear.

▷ Perhaps you feel a sense of resistance.

▷ Perhaps you scrambled for a procrastination excuse.

▷ Perhaps you resented the idea of being told what to do.

▷ Perhaps you flatly refused even to entertain the idea of making a start.

And so on... There is an infinite number of responses available.

Completing this task is in your best interests, but a part of you wants to avoid it. This is the essence of procrastination – you are in two minds. Recognizing this experience, whenever it arises, is an important step forward.

To get a fuller picture, we need a tool for gathering information.

The ABC model

In the 1950s a clinical psychologist named Albert Ellis devised a tool for capturing our thoughts, feelings and behaviours at important times. It is known as the ABC model, and it's very simple:

▶ **Activating situation** – simply the situation you're in when procrastinating. Considerations include: where you are, what you are doing, how you feel, and what you are *supposed* to be doing.

▶ **Belief** – the thoughts running through your mind: tempting procrastination excuses leading you from the task, and deeper thoughts revealing your (often distorted) beliefs about taking action. Thoughts can be verbal or visual in nature, for example: *mental pictures of tempting procrastination activities.*

▶ **Consequences** – the emotions and behaviours resulting from our thoughts; e.g. feelings of stress or reluctance, and avoidance behaviours.

Recording your thoughts, feelings and behaviours *while procrastinating* means you can then learn to change them. Let's see the ABC model in action – it's very straightforward. We'll focus on activating situations to begin.

Case study: Ruth's story

Ruth, a massage therapist from London, has been in business for just over a year. She loves working closely with people and enjoys the freedom of being self-employed. However, there are problems.

Ruth frequently procrastinates, especially when marketing her business. Also, she is very disorganized. Bills go unpaid, professional memberships lapse, and she finds it difficult to return phone calls. Although Ruth loves being a therapist, she admits her business is failing.

Ruth was given some very simple forms, known as 'ABC records', to fill out. Whenever she found herself procrastinating, she made notes about the situation. Here are her answers:

Date and time:	10 May, 7 p.m.
Activating situation:	*What task did procrastinate about?* *Answering emails from clients.* *At the moment you procrastinated, where were you?* *In my office, sitting at my desk.* *Were you finding it difficult to start a task/persevere with a task/complete a task/or get going again in between tasks?* *Start a task.* *What was your emotional state just before procrastinating, and why?* *Tired after a busy day, but quite happy and relaxed.* *What was the very last thing you thought, felt or did, before you got the urge to procrastinate?* *I turned on my laptop and opened Internet Explorer. Straight away I got the urge to check Facebook.* *Who else was involved, and why?* *The clients who sent me emails.* *Procrastination type – was it: denial, refusal or delay?* *Refusal? I sat down to check my emails, and the next thing I know I'm on Facebook!!*

As we can see from Ruth's first ABC record, she *refused* (albeit not consciously) to check her emails and instead opened Facebook. She procrastinated with *low awareness* – without the ABC record it may have gone unnoticed.

Her problem could be *habitual*. In response to a *cue* – opening the web browser – she felt an urge to log into Facebook. It might also be emotional; Ruth does not seem confident when dealing with business matters.

Let's review Ruth's second ABC record table:

Date and time:	12 May, 10.30 a.m.
Activating situation:	*What task did you procrastinate about* *Setting off for a meeting.* *Were you finding it difficult to start a task / persevere with a task / complete a task / or get going again in between tasks?* *Start a task (as in, getting out of the door!)* *At the moment you procrastinated, where were you?* *At home, in my kitchen.* *What was your emotional state just before procrastinating, and why?* *Stressed! I was running very late.* *What was the very last thing you thought, felt or did, before you got the urge to procrastinate?* *I turned on my laptop and started checking emails.* *Who else was involved, and why?* *My friend, Tom, who'd agreed to help me with some marketing for my business.* *Procrastination type – was it: denial, refusal or delay?* *Delay! I didn't understand why and it was VERY upsetting.*

In this example, we can see that Ruth procrastinated by delaying. Instead of leaving for her meeting, she started a less important activity. She was aware that she was procrastinating, and it caused her distress.

Note: Ruth procrastinated by answering emails – a task previously avoided. As we discussed earlier, procrastination is a complex matter. Here is her final example:

Date and time:	13 May, 10.30 a.m.
Activating situation:	*What task did you procrastinate about?* Sorting through a pile of papers. *Were you finding it difficult to start a task / persevere with a task / complete a task / or get going again in between tasks?* Start a task. *At the moment you procrastinated, where were you?* In my flat. *What was your emotional state just before procrastinating, and why?* Relaxed. It was my day off. *What was the very last thing you thought, felt or did, before you got the urge to procrastinate?* Walked past a pile of paperwork in the corner of my living room, and switched on my laptop. I thought, 'I haven't got time.' *Who else was involved, and why?* Nobody. *Procrastination type – was it: denial, refusal or delay?* Refusal. Looking back, I remember seeing them and deciding to sort through it later.

Here, Ruth rejected the idea of an unpleasant job and quickly focused elsewhere. This is a clear example of refusal, and it took just moments.

Notice the level of detail in Ruth's answers; she has tried to be thorough and give *context*. When you make your own notes, imagine writing them for somebody else – include relevant points and useful detail.

Completing these ABC records improved Ruth's awareness; she noticed the common thread running through her examples – they were all business-related, and involved her laptop. She then knew to be more vigilant in similar situations.

So – now it's your turn. Although simple, this next exercise is important. Remember: any urge to gloss over this exercise is just an invalid signal from your brain.

EXERCISE: GETTING TO KNOW YOUR ACTIVATING SITUATIONS

▶ This exercise takes just a few minutes each time.

▶ The aim of the exercise it to record your experience when you find yourself procrastinating.

▶ Use your notebook, or photocopied ABC records (see Figure 3.1 below), to record the requested information.

▶ Carry this out multiple times over the next few days. Complete this exercise ten times before moving on to the next chapter.

1 For the next few days, pay close attention when procrastinating. You might not even notice at first, so *check in* with yourself and ask:

▷ 'Am I in denial about an important task?'

▷ 'Have I just rejected the idea of doing something?'

▷ 'Am I just delaying here?'

▷ 'What am I actually doing?'

2 Whenever you procrastinate, make notes about the *activating situation*. Write down the date and time, and then answer the following questions:

▷ *What task are you procrastinating about?* At that moment, what *should* you have been doing instead? If you should be doing lots of things, list the important tasks. Do not dismiss examples because they feel trivial – take note whenever you procrastinate.

▷ *Were you finding it difficult to start a task / persevere with a task / complete a task / or get going again in between tasks?* Knowing when you are prone to procrastination helps.

▷ *At the moment you starting procrastinating, where were you?* Note where you were at the time. Be specific, e.g. 'in the kitchen area at work' rather than 'in work'.

▷ *What was your emotional state just before procrastinating, and why?* Our emotional state is often relevant. Note it and explain why you felt this way. Pay extra attention to tiredness, stress and complacency. For example:

1 'I was relaxed, watching the TV – I had loads of time left!'

2 'I was stressed – this deadline is really close.'

3 'I was reluctant to do anything, I felt so tired.'

4 'I felt discouraged. I didn't know where to start.'

▷ *What was the very last thing you thought, felt or did, before you got the urge to procrastinate?* Identify the *preceding action* – the very last thing you thought or did before procrastinating. You may have to work backwards to remember. Pay extra attention when computers, phones, game consoles, or TVs are involved. For example:

1 'I took a little break.'

2 'I was sitting down, and thought about exercising.'

3 'I was on my laptop, and I opened Internet Explorer.'

4 'I walked past the kitchen, and saw the dirty dishes.'

5 'I sat down at my desk in work, and thought about writing the report.'

6 'I thought about doing something, and didn't know where to start.'

7 'I was overwhelmed by the amount of work I have on my plate.'

8 'I sat on the settee, and turned on the TV.'

▷ *Who else was involved, and why?* Our tasks often involve other people, at least indirectly. Are you completing a task for somebody else? For example:

1 'My boss – he set me this task.'

2 'My partner – he'd asked me to run the errand.'

3 'The sales team – I had to write a report for them by Monday.'

4 'My clients – they'd sent me the emails.'

5 'My mum – I was said I would call.'

▷ *Procrastination type – was it: denial, refusal or delay?*
It helps to understand the type of procrastination you experienced. Consider the process you went through and the point you arrived at:

1 Ignoring a task is denial.

2 Rejecting a task, after thinking about it fleetingly, is refusal.

3 Focusing on a task, but feeling unable to make progress, is delay.

And that is all you need to do. Spend *a couple of minutes* making brief notes each time. This information will prove invaluable.

Figure 3.1 is an ABC record for you to photocopy or otherwise reproduce.

Alternatively, use your notebook, writing out the headers as follows:

Date and time:

Task:

Stage (starting, finishing, etc.):

Where:

Emotional state:

Preceding action:

Who else involved:

Type (denial, refusal, delay):

Date and time:	
Activating situation:	*What task did you procrastinate about?*
	Were you finding it difficult to start a task / persevere with a task / complete a task / or get going again in between tasks?
	At the moment you procrastinated, where were you?
	What was your emotional state just before procrastinating, and why?
	What was the very last thing you thought, felt or did, before you got the urge to procrastinate (the preceding action)?
	Who else was involved, and why?
	Procrastination type – was it: denial, refusal, or delay?

Figure 3.1 Blank ABC record

This information would take up one page in an A5 notebook.

Complete this exercise *at least* ten times before moving on to the next chapter. It only takes a few minutes. You will benefit because:

▶ You will learn about your procrastination.

▶ Your state of mind will change, alleviating stress.

▶ Exercises later in this book will make more sense.

Remember: at this stage, you are not trying to stop procrastinating. Be mindful of the following thoughts:

▶ 'I don't need to do this exercise – I can beat procrastination without it.'

▶ 'I don't want to do this exercise; I'll just read on.'

▶ 'It'll be too difficult – I'm scared just thinking about it.'

▶ 'I will come back to it, just not yet...'

These are just *procrastination excuses* – ignore them. Try something different this time. Complete the exercise, and things will start to change.

Moving on

Go about your normal life for a few days, and note your observations whenever you procrastinate. Also, reread your goal worksheet and your action plan. Think about starting it, and make notes if this causes you to procrastinate.

In the meantime, here are some Focus points:

▶ You are not a singular entity. Most of your brain's activity is unconscious to you; and some of these processes override your conscious control. This is why we procrastinate.

▶ Label procrastination urges as 'faulty signals'. They are not you; they are just created by your brain.

▶ We often procrastinate with little or no awareness. Check in with yourself frequently, and ask these questions:

▷ 'Am I in denial about an important task?'

▷ 'Have I just rejected the idea of doing something?'

▷ 'Am I just delaying here?'

▷ 'What am I actually doing?'

The ABC model is an excellent tool for gathering information. Learn to recognize *activating situations* when you procrastinate.

Remember: complete the 'Getting to know your activating situations' exercise ten times before moving on to the next chapter. This won't take long, but you'll gain useful insights into your behaviour.

Next step

We will collate your results in Chapter 4. In the meantime, get to grips with the exercises in this chapter. The first steps are often the most difficult, but also the most important. Good luck!

Getting the full picture

In this chapter you will learn:

▶ *How to get to know your procrastination 'cues' – including the associated tasks, emotions, locations and people*

▶ *To use the 'ABC model' to provide further insights into your procrastination*

▶ *How we use procrastination excuses, activities and pay-offs to justify our procrastination*

▶ *How to use a 'Procrastination fact sheet' to provide a summary of our observations.*

How do you feel?

1 Are you aware when you procrastinate?

2 Do you tell yourself: 'I'll do it tomorrow'?

3 Do you wonder why you waste so much time?

4 Do you excuse yourself from taking action?

5 Do you wish you could take more responsibility for your actions?

In Chapter 3 you were encouraged to gather information. Let's collate that information into something useful. By building up a profile of your procrastination, you will learn to recognize when you are at risk.

Did you complete the ten ABC records from the previous chapter? You will need that information before continuing.

Before we start, let's discuss one of the more interesting aspects of human psychology.

Cognitive dissonance

As mentioned previously, our minds are not singular. We carry within us different beliefs, desires, values and fears. Sometimes, these various elements *clash*. Caught in two minds, our impulses contradict our hopes and ideals.

This is known as *cognitive dissonance*, and it bears particular relevance to procrastination.

Case study: Laura's story

Laura, a bank clerk in her twenties, hoped to lose weight for her holiday. She spent her time reading about diets, planning healthy meals, and fantasizing about her 'beach body'. It was a minor obsession.

Even though Laura yearned to lose weight, she constantly overate. Large portions at mealtimes, 'office cakes' in the afternoon, guilty snacking at night... She just could not resist, and it was making her miserable.

Some of her friends thought: 'Well, she's obviously not serious!' But judging Laura's behaviour in this way misses the point. Who does not have conflicting desires, habits and needs? And, in Laura's case, at certain times or in particular situations, her *urge to eat* was too strong to resist.

Laura was deeply unhappy, particularly as she gave in to her cravings. At such times, she would think to herself:

    ▷ 'It's OK, I'll start properly tomorrow.'

    ▷ 'I'll still have time to lose the weight.'

    ▷ 'I'm too tired to stop now.'

    ▷ 'I've overeaten already today, I'll start properly tomorrow.'

    ▷ 'Just this once. It will be OK.'

And eventually:

    ▷ 'Losing weight doesn't really matter anyway... I'm OK the way I am.'

Laura did not *really* believe these excuses, but she found dieting too stressful. Despite what she knew logically, a part of her had other ideas. Does that sound familiar?

So why couldn't Laura just stop eating? To understand her difficulties fully, we need to explore the relationship between: 'the cue', 'the excuse' and 'the pay-off'.

Getting to know your cues

Previously, you learned about the ABC model and were encouraged to make notes about your procrastination. You will need those notes to hand for this next exercise.

EXERCISE: IDENTIFYING CUES

▶ This exercise takes just a few minutes.

▶ The aim of the exercise it to identify important factors (cues) that lead to procrastination.

1 To begin, look through your ABC records and identify recurring factors.

    ▷ **What tasks did you procrastinate about?** Did you frequently procrastinate about the same *type* of task?

If a task appears three times or more in your ABC records, make a note of it. Examples might include: 'trying to write an essay', 'avoiding returning phone calls', 'cooking a meal', 'exercising', 'getting on with your job', etc. These are your **task-based cues.** (Remember to update the 'procrastination checklist' in Chapter 1 with any new insights about your procrastination.)

▷ **Were you more likely to procrastinate at a certain time?** If you procrastinated at the same time on three or more occasions, make a note of this, too. Examples might include 'between 3 p.m. and 4 p.m.', 'in the afternoon', 'after lunch', 'in the evenings', etc. These are your **time-based cues.**

▷ **Did location play a part in your procrastination?** If you procrastinated in the same location three times or more, make a note of this. Examples: 'sat on my settee at home', 'using the computer', 'at my desk in the office', etc. These are your **location-based cues.**

▷ **At which point did you procrastinate?** If you procrastinated at the same point on three occasions or more, make a note. Examples: 'starting tasks', 'completing tasks', 'making the transition from one task to the next', etc. These are your **stage-based cues.**

▷ **Were you in a particular emotional state when you procrastinated?** If the same emotional state cropped up three times or more, make a note of it. Examples: 'confused', 'lethargic', 'anxious', 'stressed', 'frustrated', 'pessimistic', 'optimistic', etc. These are your **emotion-based cues.**

▷ **Before the urge to procrastinate, what was the very last thing you thought or did?** If the same *type* of thought or action appears three times or more, make a note of it. Examples: 'made a cup of tea', 'opened Internet browser', 'felt discouraged because I didn't know where to start', 'thought about going to the gym', etc. These are your **preceding action cues.**

▷ **Who else was involved?** Was anybody else involved when you procrastinated – either directly or indirectly? If the same person (or group of people) crops up three times or more, make a note of this. Example: 'my boss', 'my partner', etc. These are your **people-based cues.**

▷ **Read through your ABC records, and add up the number of times you *denied* action, *refused* action, or *delayed* over action, and record the scores for each.**

2 Next, read through your answers and look for *patterns*. What situations do you need to be wary of? For the next few days, pay extra attention when you encounter these cues again.

Do not worry if no pattern emerges just yet. We will continue to look and gain awareness of your procrastination. More on that later.

!

Focus points

✳ *Cognitive dissonance is the stressful experience of being in two minds.* We find it frustrating because our immediate thoughts are inconsistent with our hopes or ideals.

✳ *Because cognitive dissonance can feel so unpleasant,* we seek to justify or excuse our behaviour.

✳ *Recognizing the cues associated with our procrastination* helps us to predict when we're at risk.

Next, let's discuss *procrastination excuses*, *procrastination activities* and *pay-offs*.

How do you excuse procrastination?

Earlier, we discussed *cognitive dissonance* – where our thoughts or actions run contrary to our values and ideals. This will be a familiar state: you want to get something done, but your thoughts and feelings stop you.

At such times, we search for a get-out clause. Remember how Laura permitted herself to overeat:

▶ 'It's OK, I'll start properly tomorrow.'

▶ 'I'll still have time to lose the weight.'

- 'I'm too tired to force myself to stop, I'll start tomorrow.'

- 'I've overeaten already today – what's the point in stopping myself now?'

- 'This food is too nice! Just this once...'

Laura would be too ashamed to share these thoughts with other people, but they solve the problem of being caught *in two minds*. Thoughts such as these are known as 'procrastination excuses'. To overcome procrastination, you must learn to recognize and dismiss them.

YOUR INNER DIALOGUE

Thinking is a continuous activity. One thought flows into the next. Sometimes focused, and at other times jagged, our thoughts reflect our mood. We identify and reason, and compare and contrast; we chatter and wonder, and we worry and fret. Thinking is an ongoing, involuntary experience. Our minds are never still.

We often think visually – images and memories flashing through our mind. Sometimes we think in words – our 'inner voice' buzzing away, providing a running commentary. Our thoughts can also seem like feelings – a derived understanding based on our emotional state.

Unless we make the effort, we do not control our thoughts. Often, they make little rational sense. Despite this, we rarely stop to think: 'Hang on, these are just thoughts!' Instead, we tend to go along with them.

Procrastination excuses are just thoughts. They seem plausible, and we're quick to believe them. However, procrastination excuses detach us from reality. At the point of delay, we have acted against our best interests. We were *looking* for the get-out clause, despite the difficulties likely to follow.

Learn to recognize and dismiss procrastination excuses, and you'll achieve more with your life. This is a very important skill to master.

Read through the list of common procrastination excuses below. Which ones do you recognize? Remember – these excuses can be verbal, visual or almost entirely emotional – a gut feeling which you then translate in your mind:

▶ Some people will *hear* these excuses. Their *inner voice* will state: 'I'm too tired, let's tackle this later' or 'I'll just make a cup of tea first.'

▶ *Others may visualize* their excuses – mental imagery of tempting alternatives, or reasons to delay.

▶ Sometimes, people *feel* their excuses, without thinking them clearly. At such times, turn these emotions into thoughts by asking: 'What are my thoughts about this?'

Procrastination excuses – and our thoughts in general – can be a combination of our inner voice, visual imagery and emotional impulses *at the same time*.

Let's go through the list. Procrastination excuses fall into three broad categories: *it's impossible*, *there's a tempting alternative*, and *it's non-obligatory*.

1 **Impossibility:**

▷ 'I don't have the motivation to do this right now.'

▷ 'I just can't be bothered!'

▷ 'I haven't got enough time; I'll start when...'

▷ 'I'm too busy to do this now, because...'

▷ 'I'll do it in a bit.'

▷ 'I'm too tired to do this now; I'll start it later.'

▷ 'I'm too stressed to do this now; I'll start later.'

▷ 'I don't know what to do next; I'll have a break and come back to it.'

▷ 'I don't know where to start; I'll have a break and come back to it.'

▷ 'I haven't got everything I need; I'll start when...'

2 Tempting alternatives:

▷ 'I will do it; I'll just do this other thing first...'

▷ 'If I leave it now, *he* or *she* will do it instead.'

▷ 'I'll leave this for now, but I promise I'll make up for it later.'

▷ 'It's not as important as *this other thing*; I'll do it later...'

3 Non-obligatory:

▷ 'I'll do it tomorrow!'

▷ 'I don't need to do this yet, because...'

▷ 'It's not a priority right now.'

▷ 'I work best when I'm under pressure – I'll wait for now.'

▷ 'It will all be fine!'

▷ 'Doing this now will make no difference anyway.'

Perhaps you have your own procrastination excuses. If so, make a note of them.

No matter what you tell yourself, and even when your excuses sound plausible and seductive – they are just *self-comforting fantasies*. You may wish to believe them, but you sabotage yourself in doing so. You will have your own variations, but all procrastination excuses reduce down to:

▶ ' It's not possible to do this yet, because...'

▶ 'I don't have to do this yet, because...'

▶ 'It's OK to do this other thing first.'

Remember – these are just *thoughts*, not reality.

WHAT'S MY EXCUSE?

We sometimes procrastinate without explicitly excusing it. We still believe action is not possible or required, but the process unfolds without conscious thought. If you find yourself procrastinating (or about to procrastinate), and you don't recall excusing yourself from taking action, ask the following question:

How am I excusing myself from doing this?

This simple question brings procrastination excuses into focus. At this point, you have to either justify your procrastination, or reveal the true reason for it. Remember: our excuses seem plausible, but they are an exercise in self-deception.

It might be true that you 'don't know where to start' or that you 'don't have enough time to complete the task'. Even so, you can *still* act towards your best interests; you can decide where to start, or make good use of the time remaining. Procrastination is never our only option.

Focus points

Thinking is a continuous and involuntary activity. Our minds are never still. One thought flows into the next.

We think in pictures and words. Visual images or memories flash through our mind, and we hear our inner voice as it 'thinks'.

Thoughts are just thoughts – they are not real. Instead of questioning their veracity, we accept them as correct or valuable. Often, our thoughts make little sense.

When we want to procrastinate, we come up with excuses. As they often contain nuggets of truth, we are quick to accept them.

Procrastination excuses fall into three broad categories: 'it's impossible', 'there is a tempting alternative', and 'it's non-obligatory'. Our excuses are just thoughts, but they have the power to detach us from reality.

Later, we will explore techniques to dismiss excuses when they arise. Before we get to that, let's turn our attention to procrastination activities.

What do you do when you procrastinate?

When we procrastinate, we usually do something else instead. It could be pleasurable – listening to music, phoning a friend, or just daydreaming. It could be distracting – for example, completing a less important task or writing a complex 'to-do' list. We can even procrastinate by excessively worrying about procrastination! The possibilities are endless.

Read through the following list of common procrastination activities. Which ones do you recognize?

Enjoyable activities:

- Watching films, TV, DVDs
- Reading books, magazines, newspapers
- Surfing the Internet
- Browsing YouTube
- Listening to music
- Playing computer games
- Going shopping
- Enjoying or reading about hobbies

Social activities:

- Seeing friends or family
- Making phone calls or sending texts
- Going out
- Spending time on social networking sites

Less important tasks:

- Completing paperwork
- Tidying the house
- Checking emails
- 'Researching' related topics online
- Sorting through paperwork
- 'Organizing' things
- Exercising
- Attending to personal grooming

Distractions:

- Eating
- Nail-biting
- Worrying about problems
- Drinking
- Taking drugs
- Staring into space

- Smoking
- Doing the opposite of my goal (e.g. eating instead of dieting)

Daydreaming and relaxing:

- Thinking about the past or future
- Imagining a better life
- Daydreaming about completing the task
- Sitting or lying down, thinking
- Coming up with plans and 'to-do' lists
- Going for a walk

These activities are only a problem when they constantly steal your time. Understand: this book is not focused on sucking the fun out of your life. The aim is to free up *more time* for guilt-free pleasure and relaxation.

Procrastination pay-offs

We procrastinate because we find it *rewarding*.

That might seem difficult to digest. Procrastination is frustrating and causes great difficulty. However – it rewards us in several ways, not least because it *provides a temporary relief from stress*. This might lead to a different kind of stress, but your brain has decided it is willing to pay the price.

Additionally, procrastination activities are usually tempting and enjoyable. Combine these two factors, and procrastination becomes highly addictive. So, read through the following list and review these basic pay-offs. Which ones seem familiar to you?

Common procrastination pay-offs:

- Relieve boredom, anxiety or frustration
- Take a small break
- Enjoy some social contact
- Satisfy hunger or thirst
- Boost comfort

- Boost energy

- Avoid difficult circumstances

- Express resentment to others

- Have fun

Add your own examples.

Although irrational, procrastination is not *baseless*. Identifying the pay-off might require some thought, but you will benefit. For example:

- If you keep interrupting work to snack – are you really hungry or just looking for comfort?

- If you keep sending texts when trying to write an important email – are you avoiding the anxiety associated with the task?

And so on. Consider the *subtext* of your actions when procrastinating. What is the deeper motivation? Be honest with yourself. By identifying the *pay-offs*, you can learn to anticipate your urges to procrastinate.

Getting the full picture

Having introduced procrastination *excuses*, *activities* and *pay-offs* – now let's gather more information. Again, at this stage, you only need to observe your procrastination. Later, we can start to change it.

EXERCISE: GETTING THE FULL PICTURE

- This exercise takes just a few minutes each time.

- The aim of the exercise it to record your experience when you procrastinate.

- Use your notebook, or photocopied ABC records, to record the requested information.

- Carry this out several times over the next few days. Complete ten ABC records before moving on.

1 For the next few days, pay close attention when you procrastinate. You might not even notice you're procrastinating at first, so *check in* with yourself and ask:

   ▷ 'Am I in denial about an important task?'

   ▷ 'Have I just rejected the idea of doing something?'

   ▷ 'Am I just delaying here?'

   ▷ 'What am I actually doing?'

2 Whenever you procrastinate, make notes about the activating situation. Write down the date and time, and answer the following questions:

   ▷ What task are you procrastinating about?

   ▷ Were you finding it difficult to start a task/persevere with a task/complete a task/or get going again in between tasks?

   ▷ What was the very last thing you thought or did before you got the urge to procrastinate?

   ▷ Procrastination type – was it denial, refusal or delay?

3 We still need to ascertain important cues associated with your procrastination. Consider the following factors, and write down anything noteworthy:

   ▷ At the moment you started procrastinating, where were you?

   ▷ What was your emotional state just before procrastinating, and why?

   ▷ Who else was involved, and why?

4 Note anything new, or when clear patterns emerge. For instance, you may always procrastinate in a certain location, or when particular people are involved.

5 Then, answer the following questions thoroughly:

   ▷ *How did you excuse your decision to procrastinate. What did you say, picture or feel?*

   Make a note whenever excuse yourself from taking action. Your procrastination excuses may be verbal, visual or emotional in nature. To identify procrastination excuses, ask yourself: 'How am I excusing myself from doing this?' Write down your answer, whatever it might be.

▷ *What procrastination activity did you do instead?*

What did you do while procrastinating? Something fun? Less important 'work'? When you procrastinate, note how you spend your time.

▷ *How might procrastination have rewarded you?*

When you procrastinated, what pay-off were you seeking? Was it to have a break? To relieve stress? Were you in need of some fun? Did you wish to avoid difficult circumstances? Consider the *subtext* of your actions, and be honest with yourself.

As with the fact-finding exercise in Chapter 3, you're just observing your procrastination. Relax, take your time and be thorough. Imagine you're conducting an experiment – nothing more. Complete ten ABC records before carrying on with the rest of this book.

Figure 4.1 is a blank ABC record for you to photocopy or otherwise reproduce.

Alternatively, use your notebook and write out the headers as follows:

Date and time:

Task:

Stage (starting, finishing, etc.):

Type (denial, refusal, delay):

Cues (e.g. emotions):

Excuse:

Activity:

Pay-off:

Date and time:	
Activating situation:	*What task did you procrastinate about?*
	Were you finding it difficult to start a task / persevere with a task / complete a task / or get going again in between tasks?
	What was the very last thing you thought or did, before you got the urge to procrastinate (the preceding action)?
	Procrastination type – was it denial, refusal or delay?
	Were there any noteworthy cues (location, emotional state, other people)?
Belief:	*How did you excuse your decision to procrastinate. What did you say, picture or feel?*
Consequence:	*What procrastination activity did you do (or were you about to do) instead?*
	What pay-off might procrastinating have achieved?

Figure 4.1 Blank ABC record

This information would take up one page in an A5 notebook.

If you struggle for motivation, reread the exercise from Chapter 2: 'How much time do I really have?' And remember, answering these questions takes just minutes.

In Chapter 2, we read about Maya's difficulties with procrastination. Here is one of her ABC records. Refer to this example if you're not sure what to do.

MAYA'S ABC RECORD

Date and time:	11 June, 3 p.m.
Activating situation:	*What task did you procrastinate about?* Stuying a course module for my photography course. *Were you finding it difficult to start a task / persevere with a task / complete a task / or get going again in between tasks?* Complete a task. *Procrastination type – was it denial, refusal or delay?* Delay. *What was the very last thing you thought or did before you got the urge to procrastinate?* I thought 'This is too annoying!' *Were there any noteworthy cues (location, emotional state, other people)?* Sat at desk (as usual). Frustrated - I didn't know what to do next.
Belief:	*How did you excuse your decision to procrastinate. What did you say, picture or feel?* I said to myself, 'I can do this later. It doesn't need to be handed in for three weeks anyway.'
Consequence:	*What procrastination activity did you do instead?* Walking. *What pay-off might procrastinating have achieved?* Not sure. I think it helped me to relax.

It took Maya a couple of minutes to answer these questions. There is some useful information here:

▶ She procrastinated in the 'usual' place.

▶ She felt frustrated at the time.

▶ She excused herself by pretending the task was non-obligatory: 'I can do this later. It doesn't need to be handed in for three weeks.'

▶ Procrastinating helped her relax (although, as her deadline approaches, she will regret it).

These insights may seem obvious, but we do not always *see the wood for the trees*. A deeper understanding of procrastination helps to change it. Spend a couple of days living your life, and complete this exercise whenever you procrastinate. It *will* prove helpful.

Accepting responsibility

Assuming personal responsibility is not easy. Thoughts and feelings can overwhelm us, and procrastination *just seems* to happen.

And yet, only by accepting responsibility can you change. Consider yourself a victim of circumstance, or of your own impulses, and you disempower yourself. There *are* things which can be done. Learn small skills, in the right order, and you will significantly reduce your procrastination. It starts with the decision to take control.

Quick fix: Start small

If you're feeling overwhelmed with the exercises so far, perhaps you need to *start small*.

So, whenever you catch yourself procrastinating, spend just *two minutes* on the exercises. You may then decide to carry on, and that's fine. But, even if you don't, the next time you procrastinate complete another two minutes' worth. You'll soon get into the habit of it.

Then, try for three or four minutes. You can fully complete an ABC record in five minutes – so you'll be well on your way. With practice, it becomes much easier.

For the next couple of days, whenever you procrastinate, complete the information-gathering exercise from this chapter. Identify relevant cues, and record your procrastination excuses and activities. Next we will collate this information.

EXERCISE: UNDERSTANDING MORE ABOUT YOUR PROCRASTINATION

▶ This exercise takes 5–10 minutes.

▶ Complete this exercise when you have ten new ABC records from this chapter. You will need them to hand.

▶ The aim of this exercise is to understand your procrastination in more detail.

1 Earlier in this chapter, you completed the 'Identifying cues' exercise – you wrote down recurrent factors identified in your ABC records from Chapter 3. Now, repeat that exercise using the ABC records from *this* chapter. Follow the same instructions, and record anything which appears three times or more *across both sheets* (i.e. when the results are added together). Do that now, and read through the results.

* * * * *

2 Welcome back. Previously, we looked at procrastination *excuses*, *activities* and *pay-offs*. Next, read through your new set of ABC records, and collate the following information:

▷ **Procrastination excuses:** How did you excuse your procrastination? Read through the list of excuses earlier in this chapter, and make a list of any that seem similar. Write your own answers if required.

▷ **Procrastination activities:** What did you do when procrastinating? Again, go back to the list of procrastination activities earlier in this chapter and make a list of any that seem similar.

▷ **Procrastination pay-offs:** What was the intended pay-off? Review the pay-offs listed earlier in this chapter, and make a list of any you recognize.

Once the information from *both* sets of ABC records has been collated, you now have an overview of:

▶ common cues associated with your procrastination

▶ typical procrastination excuses

▶ typical procrastination activities

▶ the intended pay-offs.

For many, this information will be clear and concise. They will procrastinate over the same tasks, in the same locations, using the same excuses, and so on. For some, it may still seem a bit fuzzy. Even so, you still have *some* idea of the cues, the excuses and the procrastination activities that crop up. Forewarned is forearmed, and we can put this information to good use.

Your 'Procrastination fact sheet'

There is one last task to complete before moving on. Now we have collated this information, you need to be able to *see* it. This will warn you of the risks and help you avoid low-awareness procrastination.

The following exercise creates a summary of your procrastination. When complete, pin it together with your goal worksheet and action plan from Chapter 2. In addition, pin up a copy where you do most of your procrastinating if possible.

To understand what you're aiming for, here is Maya's 'Procrastination fact sheet'. She pinned this up in several places, including where she procrastinated the most – by her computer.

PROCRASTINATION FACT SHEET

Procrastination risks. I need to be careful:

Tasks: *When studying course modules for my course.*

Time: *Especially in the afternoons.*

Stage: *When completing tasks.*

Location: *When sitting at my workstation.*

Emotions: *When I feel tired, frustrated, confused.*

Preceding actions: *When I don't know what to do next. When I want to go for a walk or take a break.*

Type: *When refusing to do tasks or delaying them.*

Excuses, activities and pay-offs. Look out for:

Excuses: *I can do this later. I don't need to do this yet. Let's just have a break - I'll be able to concentrate better then.*

Activities: *Going for a walk. Browsing the Internet. Eating and drinking.*

Pay-offs: *Relieve frustration. Take a break.*

Maya's procrastination reduced significantly because this information was visible. Whenever she had the urge to procrastinate, she told herself: 'These are just false signals created by my brain. I'll enjoy resting even more when I've finished this module.' This proved highly effective.

Maya knew to be especially vigilant when tasks were difficult or frustrating. And when she found herself aimlessly browsing the Internet, it became easier to snap out of it. Her increased awareness curtailed much of the time-wasting, and she made good progress. So, now it's your turn.

EXERCISE: YOUR PROCRASTINATION 'FACT SHEET'

▶ This exercise takes just 5 minutes.

▶ The aim of this exercise is to summarize your procrastination 'warning signs'.

1 Copy your collated answers onto a single sheet of A4 paper, using the relevant headings – i.e. where cues appear three times or more. Ignore the headings with little or no relevance.

2 Always include the headings: *Tasks*, *Emotions* and *Location*, plus procrastination *Excuses*, *Activities* and *Pay-offs*.

3 Write your answers in sentence format – follow Maya's example, above.

It is a very simple task. Here is an idea of the layout, listing each *potential* heading:

PROCRASTINATION FACT SHEET

Procrastination risks. I need to be careful:

Tasks:

Time:

Location:

Stage:

Emotions:

Preceding actions:

People:

Type:

Excuses, activities and pay-offs. Look out for:

Excuses:

Activities:

Pay-offs:

You only need to use headings relevant to your procrastination.

4 When you have your fact sheet (handwritten is OK, typed up is better), pin it up with your goal worksheet and action plan.

5 Familiarize yourself with procrastination cues, the excuses you use, the procrastination activities you do, and the pay-offs you seek. This information is your 'early warning system'. It alerts you to the dangers of procrastination.

This 'Procrastination fact sheet' is helpful in several ways. Completing it before moving on is strongly recommended. To make things clear, here is a another example. Remember Mike from Chapter 1?

PROCRASTINATION FACT SHEET

__Procrastination risks.__ I need to be careful:

Tasks: *When loading the dishwasher, cleaning kitchen surfaces, and sweeping the kitchen floor.*

Time: *Especially in evenings and at weekends.*

Location: *When sitting on my settee. When in the kitchen.*

Stage: *When starting, when finishing, when going from one task to the next.*

Emotions: *When feeling frustrated.*

Preceding actions: *When I'm on my laptop or watching TV. When I've just finished loading the dishwasher.*

Type: *Denial, refusal and delay!!*

__Excuses, activities and pay-offs.__ Look out for:

Excuses: *I'll do it later. I don't need to do it yet. It can wait.*

Activities: *Laptop, Xbox, TV, reading.*

Pay-offs: *Resting.*

Mike pinned his fact sheet near his armchair *and* near the dishwasher. He now knew what to look out for, and his procrastination excuses seemed much less believable. The fact sheet made a difference.

Moving on

When caught in two minds, we search for a get-out clause. Our excuses then allow us to procrastinate. Understanding this enables you to *anticipate* procrastination. Completing your 'Procrastination fact sheet' will help. With greater awareness, things can change.

So, rather than racing ahead – spend time learning about your procrastination. Perhaps you haven't yet completed ten ABC records (from this chapter or the last). You may think 'I'll beat procrastination anyway'. Perhaps you're anxious about starting.

And this is why procrastination is so pernicious – taking action is difficult. But there is still time to catch up; answering questions is easy – particularly if you *start small*. Give it your best shot. In the meantime, here are some Focus points:

Focus points

✳ *Learn the 'cues'* – those factors associated with our procrastination. We can then change our responses to them.

✳ *Become more aware of procrastination excuses, activities* and *pay-offs*. You can then anticipate the urge to procrastinate.

✳ *It is not easy to accept responsibility for ourselves*. However, abdicating responsibility means relinquishing control. It does not have to be that way.

✳ *Complete the exercises in this chapter* and produce your 'Procrastination fact sheet' before moving on.

Next step

In the next chapter we will learn two simple techniques to change procrastination: *dismissing procrastination excuses and micro-planning*. In the meantime, spend some time observing your procrastination. It will be of great benefit.

Dismissing excuses

In this chapter you will learn:

- ► *A quick relaxation exercise to help you think clearly and avoid stress*
- ► *How to control your 'inner voice'*
- ► *How thoughts can have a powerful impact on our emotions and behaviours*
- ► *How to squash both verbal and visual procrastination excuses*
- ► *How to micro-plan*
- ► *How to bring all the above techniques together as you begin to challenge your procrastination and start to take control.*

How do you feel?

1 Are you easily discouraged?

2 Do you wish you could have more control over your thoughts?

3 Do you always search for a 'get out' clause?

4 Do you talk yourself into procrastinating?

5 Do you find yourself unsure where to start next?

In the previous chapter you gathered together information about your procrastination. Next, we will use that information to change the way you think. As a result, you will start having more control.

Did you complete the exercises in the previous chapter? Avoid racing too far ahead. You will make better progress by taking things slowly.

To begin, let's revisit the role our thinking plays in procrastination.

Controlling your thoughts

Thoughts, feelings and behaviours interact, forming an ever-evolving system. Think positively, and you tend towards optimism. Think negatively, and you'll experience limitation and fear.

Thoughts exist in the mind. They can be verbal or visual, rational or irrational; they include memories, ideas, opinions and calculations. Without thoughts, how would we know we exist? To an extent, they define who we are.

However, we forget thoughts can be *controlled*. Procrastination is a perfect example. We know life would improve by taking action, but instead our thoughts create reluctance and resistance. Despite their inherent irrationality, our thoughts are in control.

This needs to change. In this chapter, you will learn techniques to change two types of thoughts: your *inner voice* and *mental imagery*. Before that, you need to learn how to *relax*.

The importance of relaxation

It might seem counterintuitive, but relaxation *curtails* procrastination. A calm, relaxed focus enables rational thinking. It does not create instant motivation, but you are less likely to compulsively avoid stress.

Some people seem relaxed when they procrastinate, but this is not true relaxation. It is a facet of *denial*. Their relaxation would soon evaporate when confronted with taking action. The key is to stay focused and relaxed *while accepting what needs to be done*.

Let's learn how that can be achieved. Read through this exercise and attempt the steps. Do not rush through it. Learning how to stop, relax, and focus is an important skill.

EXERCISE: QUICK RELAXATION EXERCISE

▶ This exercise takes just a few moments.

▶ The aim is to use slow breathing and affirmations to relax your physiology.

▶ Use this technique many times over the next few days, and particularly whenever you are procrastinating.

1 To begin, breathe in slowly through your nose, mentally counting to five as you do so.

2 Then, slowly exhale through your mouth, relaxing your shoulders as you breathe out.

3 Repeat this three times. When you exhale, relax your shoulders, jaw, back, stomach and feet. These areas of the body often carry tension.

4 As you exhale, tell yourself: 'I'm becoming focused and rational.'

This exercise just takes moments, but you cannot rush through it. Also, don't expect miracles straight away – sadly, we're not calling in the masseur/masseuse. However, relaxing and focusing improve your ability to think rationally. More on that later.

For now, use this quick technique *at least* three or four times each day, and especially when you feel frustrated or anxious. Stress distorts our thinking – we just cannot think logically. Acquiring a level of relaxed focus improves this. Try the exercise once more, and then let's turn our attention to regaining control of your mind.

* * * * *

Welcome back. Feeling more relaxed? Use this exercise frequently. It will help.

Your inner voice

Let's try an experiment. Without speaking out loud, count down from 10 to 1. This is your *inner voice*, and it does your thinking for you. Learning to control it represents a major step in the right direction.

EXERCISE: FINDING YOUR INNER VOICE

▶ This exercise takes just a minute.

▶ The aim is to listen to your inner voice and notice its qualities.

▶ When attempting exercises such as these, relax and don't try too hard.

▶ Read through the exercise first and familiarize yourself with the steps.

1 Think to yourself: 'Where is my inner voice?' If needed, think it several times and take a moment to observe:

▷ Does it *seem* to come from the front of your imagination or the back?

▷ Is it coming from the left or the right?

▷ Is the voice loud or quiet?

2 Record your answers in your notebook:

▷ Front or back?

▷ Left or right?

▷ Loud or quiet?

There is no right or wrong way to answer these questions – it's *your* imagination. Repeat this exercise again. If you get stuck, count backwards from 10 without speaking. Spend a little time acquainting yourself with your thoughts.

* * * * *

How did you get on? It will be easy for some and tricky for others. Persevere with the exercise until you have found your inner voice. Even if 'spoken' thoughts are not your primary mode of expression, they will play some part.

Let's try another simple exercise. This next technique improves your ability to communicate with yourself *authentically*. This skill is important, but easy to master.

EXERCISE: FIND YOUR 'CERTAIN INNER VOICE'

> ▶ This exercise takes just a few moments.
>
> ▶ Use this exercise frequently over the next few days.
>
> ▶ Read through the steps first and familiarize yourself with the exercise.
>
> ▶ Use this exercise whenever verbalized thoughts cause procrastination.

1 Think about something you *know* to be true. A perfect example: the sun will come up tomorrow.

2 Then, without speaking out loud, think this thought in your mind; imagine 'speaking' it with certainty. Observe the *quality* of this thought as you think it, and answer the questions below:

   ▷ Does the thought come from the front of your imagination or the back?

   ▷ Does it come from the left or the right?

   ▷ Is the voice loud or quiet?

   ▷ Does the voice sound confident or timid? Certain or uncertain?

3 Next, imagine your voice sounding *really* certain. Pretend you're trying to convince somebody that the sun will come up. How would that sound in your mind:

  ▷ Is your voice louder? Clearer? Stronger?

  ▷ Does it come from a different location in your imagination?

  ▷ What difference is there when you imagine speaking with certainty?

4 Repeat Step 3 until your *inner voice* sounds really certain!

This exercise is simple: make your inner voice sound as certain as you can. You'll need this certainty in the days to come. Practise a little more before moving on to the next exercise. You will be encouraged to use it frequently. As a result, you will gain more control of your mind.

Mental imagery

Thoughts viewed in our 'mind's eye' have a strong impact on our emotions and behaviours. When mental imagery is vivid, containing *colour* and *movement*, our imagination seems to take over. At other times visual thoughts appear dull and distant. Such thoughts affect us less. We can utilize these general principles.

Learning to control your visual thoughts makes a tremendous difference to procrastination.

EXERCISE: TUNING IN TO MENTAL IMAGERY

▶ This exercise takes less than a minute.

▶ The aim is to visualize a simple picture in your mind and observe its qualities.

▶ Don't think too hard; exercises such as this one work best when you relax into them.

▶ Read through the exercise first and familiarize yourself with the steps.

1 In a moment, close your eyes and imagine *a red helium balloon* rising through the sky. Then, answer the following questions:

   ▷ Could you see the colour of the balloon (in your imagination)?

   ▷ Was the balloon moving?

   ▷ Which detail(s) stood out the most?

2 Next, close your eyes and imagine standing outside of your front door. Relax into it, and imagine opening the door. Then answer the following questions:

   ▷ Could you see the colour of the door?

   ▷ Was the door life-size, TV screen-size, or in between the two?

   ▷ Was the image focused or fuzzy?

   ▷ As you imagined opening the door, did the image move?

   ▷ Did you see yourself stood in front of the door, or were you just *there*?

   ▷ When you imagined opening your front door, what feelings did you feel (if any)?

Some people will create clear, bright images. Others may find them fuzzy, black and white, and fleeting – as if not really there. Your imagination is unique to you; there is no right or wrong way to use it.

Try the exercise again, especially Step 2. Practise making it *feel* like you are coming home. Make the door appear brighter, more focused, so you feel that you're stood in front of it. Try that now.

* * * * *

Creating mental imagery can be more challenging that hearing our inner voice. It becomes easier with practice. Try *easing* into it – you cannot force yourself to 'see' mental images. Relax, pretend the images are there – and in time they will be.

Dismissing procrastination excuses

Procrastination excuses *seem* to offer a get-out clause, but in the long run they only sabotage your progress. Your brain seeks to relieve stress or experience pleasure, but the cost is high: you miss your deadlines, abandon your goals, and let people down.

And for what? Procrastination offers only temporary respite. There will be more problems, more stress, and more *excuses* in the future. You need to inject some reality into the situation.

In the previous chapter, you noted your typical procrastination excuses. Choose one now, and run it through your mind. Then, ask yourself the following questions:

▶ *Isn't this just an excuse?*

This question pierces pretence and self-deception. If you are uncertain, imagine saying this excuse to a friend – How would you feel? How would they react?

▶ *What's the motivation behind it?*

Understand what you're trying to achieve by procrastinating, and it becomes easier to consider things rationally. Answer this question, and you'll identify the pay-off.

▶ *Work on this now for just 15 minutes, and I'm improving my life – isn't that true?*

Procrastination generally relieves negative feelings, albeit at the expense of future difficulties. When we avoid procrastination, our lives generally improve. Acknowledge this fact, and it becomes easier to do something positive.

These questions help us become more considered and rational. To see this in action, let's look at another case study:

Case study: Dan's story

Dan, a 30-year-old mature student, was struggling with his dissertation. He found procrastination excuses especially difficult to deal with. Within moments of sitting down to work, Dan would say to himself: 'I'm not in the mood for this yet – I can do it later' or 'There's plenty of time to get this done – I don't need to do it now.'

These excuses contained some truth. He genuinely wasn't in the mood, and the deadline was still months away. However, Dan knew he had to make a start, otherwise he'd quickly fall behind.

He was shown how to challenge procrastination excuses. Here are his results:

Procrastination excuse:

'I'm not in the mood for this yet, we can do it later...'

Dan's challenges to this excuse:

▷ 'Isn't this just an excuse?'

If I am honest, yes it is. I never seem to be in the mood. And even if I am not in the mood – I know I still have to do the work or I'll fail my course.

▷ 'What's the motivation behind it?'

I'm tired and stressed, and I don't want to feel more tiredness and stress!

▷ 'Work on this now for just 15 minutes, and I'm improving my life – isn't that true?'

I cannot deny this is true. Yes.

To procrastinate, we have to pretend it is OK to delay or abandon a task. Our excuses may sound plausible, but logically we know the truth: we are acting against our best interests.

By asking these three questions, Dan quickly reached a point of complete honesty with himself. This one technique reduced his procrastination by about 30 per cent. That is quite an achievement, and it took just moments.

Later, we will practise with these questions. First, let's explore a technique for squashing visual procrastination excuses.

EXERCISE: CHANGING MENTAL IMAGERY

▶ This exercise takes just a few moments.

▶ The aim is to reduce the impact of negative mental imagery.

▶ Read through the exercise first and familiarize yourself with the steps.

▶ Use this exercise whenever negative mental imagery causes procrastination.

1 Are your procrastination excuses sometimes visual? If so, picture one now. Refer to your answers from the previous chapter if required. When you have the mental image in your mind, answer the following questions:

▷ Is the image colourful or black and white?

▷ Is it life-size, TV screen-size, or somewhere in between the two?

▷ Is it moving or still?

▷ Is it sharp or fuzzy?

▷ Is it bright or dull?

▷ Do you see yourself in the picture, or are you just *there*?

▷ When you run this image through your mind, what emotions do you feel?

2 Next, take a moment and change the mental imagery:

▷ Make it less colourful.

▷ Make it smaller.

▷ Make it a still image.

▷ Make it fuzzy and dim.

▷ Switch the perspective into third person (he/she) rather than first person (I).

3 Run the procrastination excuse through your mind in this new *mode*, and its impact should be negated – at least to an extent.

4 Tell yourself, using your 'certain inner voice': 'This is just an excuse. If I work on this task for just 15 minutes, I'm improving my life – isn't that true?'

It takes practice to weaken mental images in this way. You have to *catch hold* of the image and systematically change it; first remove the colour, then shrink it in size, stop the motion, change the perspective to third person, make it fuzzier, etc.

If visual procrastination excuses cause you problems, this technique should be simple and effective.

Focus points

✻ *Procrastination excuses may seem to offer an escape route*, but they only cause further problems. There will be more stress – and more excuses – in the future.

✻ *These three questions* will help you to dismiss verbal procrastination excuses:
  1 Isn't this just an excuse?
  2 What's the motivation behind it?
  3 Work on this now for just 15 minutes, and I'm removing negative feelings – isn't that true?

✻ *To procrastinate, we have to pretend that our delay will not cause problems*. Dismiss excuses, and be completely honest with yourself.

✻ *Visual procrastination excuses can be dismissed* by making them smaller, black and white, still and 3rd person. This quickly reduces the power such thoughts have over our emotions.

Micro-planning

As research clearly shows, people who *make plans* progress further than those who do not. If you know what to do next, you're more likely to make a start – and keep going.

This next exercise involves planning your actions for *just the next 15 minutes*. This helps in two ways: you know what to do next, and you'll be ready for procrastination urges when they arise. Your plan will keep you on track.

EXERCISE: GETTING A MINI-ACTION PLAN TOGETHER

- This exercise takes a couple of minutes.

- The aim is to work out how to get started, and how you'll cope with difficult moments.

- Use it before taking action.

1 In Chapter 2 you created a *goal worksheet* and *action plan*. From your action plan, select a small task you could start now. Choose something you could complete within 15 minutes, and which you would normally procrastinate about. In your notebook, describe the task in one sentence.

2 Next, read through this quick example. Mike (from Chapter 1) drew up a 'mini-action plan' to help with loading the dishwasher and cleaning his kitchen:

(A) The steps I will take:

Firstly, I will gather together all of the dishes. Then, I'll unload the dishwasher. Then, I'll add the dirty dishes to the dishwasher, add a tablet and start it going. Then I'll spray the surfaces and give them a wipe down. Then, I'll give the floors a quick sweep. Then it will be done.

As you can see: simple but comprehensive. Mike wrote down each step, using action-oriented language. Here is the rest of his plan. It is self-explanatory:

(B) How long will I be active for:

I'll clean my kitchen for 15 minutes.

(C) How I will cope with the urge to procrastinate:

I'll use the quick relaxation exercise and dismiss any procrastination excuses.

Then I'll carry on with the plan.

(D) When I might get the urge to procrastinate:

Just before I start the gathering the dishes together (delaying tactics). And before sweeping the floors. I really hate that job!

Again – very simple, but drawing up a mini-action plan *always* improves things. Now it's your turn.

3 In Step 1, you selected a task you could start now. Define each *small step* you will take, and how long you'll work for – in this case, 15 minutes. Be comprehensive.

4 Then, note how you'll cope when you get the urge to procrastinate. At this stage, the tools you have include: the 'Quick relaxation exercise' and the 'Dismissing procrastination excuses' technique.

5 Finally, decide when you're likely to feel those urges. Refer to your 'Procrastination fact sheet'. Do you struggle when starting tasks, completing tasks, or making the transition from one task to another? Does reluctance, confusion or frustration play a part?

6 When the plan is complete, read it back – out loud if possible. As you read each step, imagine you're about to undertake it.

Photocopy the blank mini-action plan in Figure 5.1, or write the headers into your notebook:

MINI-ACTION PLAN

(A) The steps I will take: _____

_____

_____

_____

(B) How long I will be active for: _____

(C) How I will cope with the urge to procrastinate: _____

_____

_____

(D) When I might get the urge to procrastinate: _____

_____

Figure 5.1 Mini-action plan

Alternatively, your notebook version could even look something like this:

MINI-ACTION PLAN

STEPS:

TIME:

COPE BY:

DANGER:

How does your plan look? It only needs to be basic, and you don't need to believe it – yet. This exercise forms a key step in your recovery from procrastination – avoid glossing over it.

Quick fix: Procrastination flash points

Procrastination is not a constant state – it grows stronger and weaker at certain points. Be vigilant, especially in these moments:

* *Before starting a task*: procrastination urges are often strongest before we start. They typically subside within 5 minutes of taking action.

* *When we don't know what to do next, or when a task becomes more difficult*: the more stressful action becomes, the greater the temptation to do something else.

* *The middle of a task*: people often flag as they approach the halfway mark, especially with arduous tasks. Get through this moment, and action quickly grows easier.

* *Towards the end of the task*: rather than seeing 'the light at the end of the tunnel', some people habitually struggle to finish tasks. At such moments, remind yourself to push on – you'll feel glad when you've finished.

* *While making the transition from one task to a next*: the temptation to take a 'little rest' is strongest when we finish a task. Hours can be 'lost' as a result. If you want a break, set a definite time limit – and stick to it.

Procrastination mostly occurs at such moments, so be especially wary.

Tying this together

If you have been following the exercises, keep the following things in mind:

▶ You have recorded information about certain *cues* – those factors associated with your procrastination. Be especially mindful at such times.

▶ You also identified the tasks you tend to procrastinate about, and whether you struggle to get going, make progress, or complete those tasks. Again – be especially vigilant.

▶ Try to catch procrastination as it starts. Remember to check in with yourself: 'Am I just delaying here? Have I just refused to do something?'

▶ You have learned to recognize procrastination excuses. Remember to ask yourself: 'How am I excusing myself from doing this?'

▶ Notice when you are engaged in *procrastination activities*. So, if you often procrastinate by aimlessly browsing the Internet – ask yourself: 'How am I excusing this?'

▶ To keep track of this, pay attention to your 'Procrastination fact sheet'. Hopefully, this is pinned where you can see it.

In addition, let's recap the techniques in this chapter. So far, you have learned:

▶ a quick-and-easy technique for relaxing away stress

▶ a question-based technique for dismissing *verbal* procrastination excuses

▶ a mental imagery technique for squashing *visual* procrastination excuses

▶ Micro-planning – creating a quick list of steps, including a time limit and contingency against procrastination urges.

These are easy skills to master, but they require practice. For the next few days, live your normal life while aiming to spot procrastination *just before it takes hold*. In particular, focus on identifying procrastination excuses when you think them.

In addition, read your goal worksheet and action plan frequently. Consider starting the tasks you've identified as part of your plan. Whenever you feel the urge to procrastinate, here's what to do:

Quick fix: Focus on preparation

When planning our next steps, sometimes we need to focus on preparation:

✳ Do you need to clean and tidy your work area?

✳ Do you need to gather information together?

✳ Are there people you need to speak to?

And so on. Spending 15 minutes on preparation can be of great benefit. Plus, by getting *up and running*, it becomes easier to keep going.

Of course, thoroughly preparing to start can become procrastination in itself. Limit your preparation time to just 15 or 30 minutes, otherwise you may just be procrastinating once more.

EXERCISE: REGAINING CONTROL

▶ This exercise takes just a few minutes each time.

▶ The aim is to notice procrastination and reassert some degree of control.

▶ Use your notebook, or photocopied ABC records, to record the requested information.

▶ Carry this out multiple times over the next few days. Complete a minimum of ten ABC records before moving on to the next chapter.

1 For the next few days, pay close attention whenever you feel the urge to procrastinate. Ideally, catch yourself before procrastination takes hold.

2 Then, make a note of the following:

▷ the time and date

▷ the task you procrastinated about

▷ your feelings towards that task

▷ any noteworthy cues (location, people involved, time of day, etc.).

As before, pinpoint the factors contributing to your procrastination. Be as thorough as possible.

3 Next, answer the following questions:

▷ What procrastination activity were you doing (or about to do) instead?

▷ How might this procrastination activity have rewarded you?

4 Then, use the quick relaxation exercise found earlier in this chapter. Even if you don't feel particularly stressed – do not skip this step!

5 How did you excuse your procrastination? Think back, or ask yourself: 'How am I excusing this?' Make a note of your procrastination excuse.

6 Then, ask yourself these three questions (or use the exercise 'Changing mental imagery' given earlier in this chapter):

▷ Isn't this just an excuse?

▷ What's the motivation behind it?

▷ Work on this now for just 15 minutes, and I'm removing negative feelings – isn't that true?

As you ask yourself these questions, remember to use your 'certain inner voice' practised earlier.

7 Then, complete the 'Getting a mini-action plan together' exercise. Write down the steps you could take for the next 15 minutes, and how you'll cope with procrastination urges. Remember to identify the moments where you are at risk of procrastinating.

8 Finally, while staying relaxed, read your mini-action plan and think about working on the task *for just 15 minutes*. If you come up with more procrastination excuses, use the techniques in this chapter to dismiss them.

At this point, one of three things may happen:

1 You might feel very stressed and bemused by your procrastination.

2 The *real* reason for your procrastination may become clear.

3 If the task is relatively straightforward, you may just get on with it and execute your mini-action plan.

Each of these outcomes is fine; you're still only practising. Practise building a relaxed focus, dismissing excuses, and writing out your mini-action plans. Anything else is a bonus. Each time you complete the exercise, use a new ABC record or your notebook to write down your results.

Figure 5.2 is a blank ABC record for you to photocopy or otherwise reproduce.

Alternatively, record this information in your notebook:

Date and time:

Task:

Feelings:

Cues:

Excuse:

Activity:

Pay-off:

Technique results:

Date and time:	
Activating situation:	*The task you procrastinated about:* *Your feelings towards that task:* *Noteworthy cues:*
Belief:	*How did you excuse your decision to procrastinate? What did you say, picture or feel?*
Consequence:	*What procrastination activity did you do (or were you about to do) instead?* *How might you have found this procrastination activity rewarding?* *What happened next? Did you feel stressed or relaxed? If you felt stressed, did you understand why? Were you able to carry out your plan?*

Figure 5.2 Blank ABC record

It won't always be necessary to write down *so much*. You're still learning, and note-taking is an important part of that process. Don't gloss over it. To build up your skills and get the most out of this chapter, complete the exercises *at least* ten times before moving on to the next.

Moving on

We've introduced tools to promote change. For the next few days, focus on learning to relax, dismissing procrastination excuses, and writing out mini-action plans. Master these steps, and you will have a firm platform to build on. Take your time. There is no point racing ahead.

In the meantime, here are some Focus points:

Focus points

* Staying focused and relaxed, while *accepting the reality* of what needs to be done, helps people overcome procrastination.
* By taking control of your thoughts, you can reconnect with reality before procrastination takes hold.
* Practise tuning into your thoughts and dismiss procrastination excuses, both verbal or visual, whenever they arise.
* Having a plan is clearly better than feeling stuck. When you catch yourself procrastinating, write out a mini-action plan covering the next 15 minutes. Read your plan back to yourself, and imagine taking each step.
* After dismissing procrastination excuses and getting a mini-action plan together, you *may* feel more motivated. If so, feel free to carry out your plan.

Next step

As before, remember to engage with these exercises before moving on. Practise what you have learned so far. In the next chapter, we will learn how *stress* causes procrastination.

Fear and frustration

In this chapter you will learn:

► *About the relationship between procrastination and stress*

► *The nature of frustration and anxiety*

► *How we become 'stuck' in our 'comfort zone'*

► *About the relationship between procrastination and limiting beliefs*

► *How to understand our negative emotions*

► *How to bring all the above techniques together as you continue to challenge your procrastination and take control.*

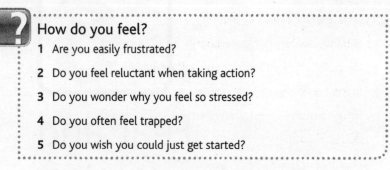

How do you feel?

1 Are you easily frustrated?

2 Do you feel reluctant when taking action?

3 Do you wonder why you feel so stressed?

4 Do you often feel trapped?

5 Do you wish you could just get started?

In the previous chapter, you learned how to dismiss procrastination excuses and get a mini-action plan together. As a result, you may have found it easier to take action. If so, well done!

However, you may have felt anxious, frustrated or *stuck*. Next, we will explore the cause of such feelings. With this understanding, you'll take another step towards overcoming procrastination.

What is stress?

Modern life is complicated, but we often fail to notice how stressful it can be. We plough on regardless, doing our best to keep it together. Naturally, this takes its toll. Let's look at this in more detail.

Stress is our response to threatening situations. Our heart pounds faster, blood pressure rises, our breath quickens, and hormone levels increase. Stress also affects us mentally and emotionally. Our thoughts become frantic, and feelings overwhelm us. We can easily spiral out of control.

At the appropriate times, stress is helpful. Sometimes it motivates us – and it's vital in dangerous situations. However, with too much stress comes exhaustion; our mood suffers, we become withdrawn, and motivation is lost. This can lead to anxiety and even depression. Chronic stress is debilitating.

Even if you procrastinate in a relaxed way, consider the role stress plays in your life. Read through the following list – which factors do you recognize?

Typical internal causes of stress:

▶ Difficulties accepting uncertainty

▶ Unrealistic expectations of yourself or others

▶ Persistent or repetitive pessimism

▶ Perfectionism

▶ Procrastination

▶ Negative self-talk

Then, consider these external causes of stress. Ask yourself whether you have experienced, or are experiencing, difficulties in any of these areas:

Typical external causes of stress:

▶ Work piling up

▶ Problems in relationships or the home

▶ Financial problems

▶ A hectic lifestyle

▶ Missed deadlines

▶ Unresolved health issues

How many factors apply to you. As you may have noticed, the internal causes of stress often *lead to* procrastination. And the external causes of stress, work piling up or financial difficulties, often *result from* procrastination. Stress is compounded from within and without.

Even if you don't feel overly stressed, the exercises in this chapter are still important – practise them thoroughly. For those who already know they're stressed, or who have just opened their eyes to the possibility, read this chapter carefully.

To begin, let's explore two major types of stress – frustration and fear.

What is frustration?

Cast your mind back to your schooldays, and imagine you're stuck inside on a sunny day. You can hear other kids shouting and having fun, while you're stuck in this stuffy classroom. As you look through the window, every inch of you yearns to play outside. This is frustration – our emotional response to *restriction*:

▶ Frustration is being unable to do what we want.

▶ Frustration is finding things difficult, boring or pointless.

▶ Frustration is the anger and disappointment we feel when we lack control.

Frustration restricts our thoughts, feelings and actions. Instead of remaining calm, clear-headed and optimistic, we find ourselves short-tempered, fuzzy-minded and unable to stay rational. Frustration interferes with our decision-making. It is inherently stressful.

To achieve anything *worthwhile*, we have to experience short-term frustration. People often struggle with this; instead, we fixate on gratification or comfort. Unfortunately, this leads to a different type of stress – the frustration of thwarted ambition. Even though *logically* we know this, it is still difficult to accept.

Frustration is subjective. One person might *hate* cleaning a kitchen, while another will give it no thought. It depends on our attitude towards the task. For some, frustration feels like an angry, restricted disappointment. For others, it is more of a braced resistance – like digging one's heels in. Perhaps you can recognize these feelings? When frustration takes over, it is very unpleasant. This is something we can learn to change.

Procrastination is a strategy for avoiding all of this. Of course, it only holds us back – for reasons explained previously. With repetition and practice, we can learn to tolerate frustration. Later, we will explore how. For now, let's look at another major cause of stress.

What is anxiety?

Anxiety is *fear*. Our heart rate increases, stress hormones are released, we sweat more, and our mouths become dry. Our stomachs churn or tingle, and we might feel shaky, tense, agitated and afraid. As you can see, anxiety and stress are physiologically similar.

Anxiety also changes our psychology: our thoughts become all-or-nothing, irrational and catastrophic. Reality is hard to grasp, and we spiral into distress. Anxiety is unhelpful because it involves an *imagined* threat. Compare these scenarios:

▶ You're driving on the motorway and a tyre bursts. You experience a sudden burst of fear, and rightly so. These physiological changes ready you for the emergency, and you quickly react. The fear is warranted and useful.

▶ You're driving on the motorway, anxious that a (perfectly fine) tyre will blow out. You feel the physiological and psychological effects of anxiety, but this *impairs* your ability to drive normally. Eventually you abandon the motorway in favour of slower roads. This unwarranted fear has proved disruptive.

In the second example, anxiety has caused an unnecessary and irrational decision. Over time, such decisions become habitual; we automatically choose behaviour designed to keep us safe. These 'safety behaviours' focus on *avoidance*. We keep to our comfort zone, hesitating instead of acting. The relationship between anxiety and procrastination should be clear.

Changing procrastination means changing your thoughts, your feelings and your actions. To achieve this, it helps to understand the nature of personal *belief*. They are the underlying cause of frustration and anxiety.

Focus points

* *Stress is a physical response to threatening situations.* At such times, our physiology changes in readiness for danger.
* *Internal causes of stress, such as negative thinking, often lead to procrastination.* By contrast, external causes of stress, such as financial difficulties, often occur because of procrastination.
* *When we experience restriction, we often feel frustrated.* People who procrastinate often find it frustrating to take action.
* *Anxiety is fear.* When we feel anxious about something, we wish to avoid it. Again, this leads to procrastination.
* *Over time, we learn to keep ourselves in our 'comfort zone'.* Procrastination, over time, becomes a difficult habit to break.

Beliefs and procrastination

Procrastination relieves stress. At least, that is what we believe. This may not be a conscious belief, and it makes no logical sense, but on some level we must believe it, otherwise why would we procrastinate?

Beliefs are contradictory, irrational and often unhelpful. By changing limiting and irrational beliefs, we free ourselves from fear and frustration – at least to some extent. It becomes easier to act logically rather than succumb to compulsive action. And procrastination *is* compulsive.

You are a complex system – a combination of thought, emotion, belief, behaviour and habitual response. These factors change your perception of yourself – and of the world around you. Your beliefs are powerful, controlling the decisions you make. They define your reality.

As a species, much of our decision-making is irrational. Logically, we *know* what we need to do to – but our beliefs exist beyond reason. They are our emotional understanding; conclusions we draw from painful experiences. And they form a prison in our mind, wrought of past failure.

Case study: Annette's story

Annette had enjoyed a long and successful career in academia. Recently retired, she was finally 'getting around' to writing her novel. She felt confident – after all, she had authored a number of academic papers over the years.

However, Annette constantly found herself avoiding her writing. Bemused and frustrated, for the first time in her life she didn't know what to do. She procrastinated in many different ways:

- ▷ Within five minutes of sitting down with her laptop, she'd find herself doing something else: tidying, eating, watching TV or daydreaming about her completed *masterpiece*.
- ▷ Whenever she had a good idea, she'd avoid writing it down – even though she carried a notepad for that very purpose.
- ▷ Annette would often sit and stare at a blank page. She'd forget the notes she *had* written, and instead wrestle with herself: 'Why can't I just write something?'
- ▷ She frequently found herself socializing instead of writing. Although she felt guilty, fun would still come first.
- ▷ Annette could not control her impulses to browse the Internet, and she'd repeatedly check her emails or log onto Facebook. At such times she would feel stuck and utterly defeated.

Perhaps you recognize some of these procrastination activities. Some of this was *denial*: e.g. 'forgetting' to write down new ideas. Sometimes, Annette was stuck in a cycle of delay, and her frustration grew intolerable.

Annette knew how to write and generally felt confident about her ideas. She eventually confided in a trusted friend and was surprised to hear herself express her deeper fears. Annette feared the novel would be mediocre at best, and that people would laugh at her for even trying. This wasn't her rational side talking; she was expressing her limiting beliefs.

Annette's confidence did not translate into optimism. She was certain it would be rejected: 'Well, It's so competitive... I just don't think I'll get anywhere with it.' Many years ago she had tried, and failed, to publish a collection of short stories.

Beyond that, Annette had to admit that she was tired. The last few years had been tough, and she liked spending more time with friends. She resented her time spent writing.

These thoughts were not often clear in her mind. Instead, she would just feel anxious or frustrated without fully understanding why. Occasionally, her fears *would* become clear, but they passed unchallenged; she just accepted them. They were her private reality.

Reading through Annette's story, we can see the following:
- ▷ Annette fears failure – she worries that her novel will be mediocre at best.
- ▷ She fears disapproval, and that other people will laugh at her for trying.
- ▷ She is pessimistic about her chances (despite having confidence in her writing).
- ▷ She is tired and prefers fun over hard work.

And here is the problem – our emotional reasoning, although irrational, distorted and often fearful, overrides our logic. Our decision-making is distorted by the need to *avoid*.

Annette was not aware of this tussle – she just found herself procrastinating. Our limiting beliefs can be as stealthy as they are powerful. But from the outside, it is easy to see why Annette struggled to write. She was torn between her ambitions and her fears.

Emotional reasoning is very powerful and can be positive. When our emotions are allied to our *best interests*, we become unstoppable. Problems only arise when we are limited by our beliefs. Invariably, we procrastinate, and we're left wondering 'Why?'

Take a moment to consider this. Think back to your desire to avoid. This is your emotional reasoning in action. It doesn't just control you; it *is* you.

Focus points

* *Beyond our logic and reason there is a deeper level of emotional belief.* It tends to be irrational, is often distorted, and leaves us prone to making illogical decisions.

* *Our emotional beliefs colour our thoughts, feelings, decisions and behaviour.* Despite this, we are not always conscious of our beliefs; they can be as stealthy as they are powerful.

* *When our beliefs are aligned to our best interests, we are unstoppable.* Athletes train regularly to achieve greatness, not because of logic but because of their emotions. 'If I do *this*, I will succeed in my goals.' Belief is key.

* *When our beliefs are opposed to our best interests, procrastination is inevitable.* In Annette's case, she felt: 'If I do *this*, then I will become a laughing stock and fail.'

Each of us has experienced the limiting effect of belief. This is especially true when struggling with procrastination. Let's review what can be done.

Limiting beliefs in action

At any given point, there will be *something* on your mind.

In the previous chapter we looked at procrastination excuses. Such excuses are accepted because they suit our need for avoidance. They are not reality, but comfortable illusions. Dismissing them is an important step.

Beyond our excuses lie our true emotional beliefs. They tend to be intransigent, consisting of *musts*, *nevers*, *shoulds* and *cannots*. Annette experienced this whenever she sat down to write, causing stress, anxiety and resistance:

▶ 'People *must* not feel bad of me.'

▶ 'I *must* not fail.'

▶ 'This *must* be perfect.'

▶ 'It's not good enough, and it *never* will be!'

These were not Annette's conscious thoughts (although they *did* pop into her mind from time to time). They are her deeper-held beliefs; they *colour* her thoughts, her perceptions, her emotions and her actions. They *caused* dim and fleeting thoughts to creep across her mind. For example:

▶ 'This is just rubbish.'

▶ 'Why can't I get this right?'

▶ 'Come on, think! This is too important to get wrong!'

▶ 'Why am I even wasting my time on this?'

Annette would also experience visual thoughts:

▶ Mental images predicting rejection letters.

▶ Bright, colourful images of her friends having fun; and then grainy, colourless images of writing alone in a gloomy room.

Such thoughts lead to stress, and the urge to procrastinate grows accordingly. Procrastination excuses inevitably follow. In full flow, procrastination is a jarring experience:

▶ We become fixated on problems, and our thinking becomes increasingly agitated and limiting.

▶ We then feel *stressed*; perhaps anxious or frustrated, perhaps defeated, resistant or deeply pessimistic.

▶ We might then start pining for more enjoyable activities, or berate ourselves for feeling 'stuck'.

At such points we need to relax, focus inwards and determine: 'What is the actual problem?' Let's explore ways to do this.

Quick fix: Don't struggle on alone

Procrastination is usually a solo pursuit. We wouldn't want other people to know – we'd be ashamed or embarrassed. Instead, we live in our heads and feel trapped by our own mind.

It always helps to get a different perspective. You may know people who procrastinate less than you. Ask them questions, and ask for advice. You don't need to bare your soul, but it does not hurt to say: 'I've been struggling to get motivated about this.' People will be happy to help. Avoid dismissing their point of view, and keep an open mind.

You *do not* have to struggle on alone.

Understanding negative emotions

To overcome procrastination, it helps to understand *why* we're procrastinating. This next exercise grants invaluable insight into our emotional reasoning.

EXERCISE: RELEASING NEGATIVE EMOTIONS

▶ This exercise takes a couple of minutes.

▶ The aim is to gain greater insight into the reasons for your procrastination.

▶ You will need a pad and paper to hand. (This also works on a computer, though it helps if you can touch-type!)

▶ Use this technique many times over the next few days, and particularly whenever you feel negative emotions about taking action.

▶ This exercise works best after using the quick relaxation exercise from Chapter 5.

▶ Read through the steps first to familiarize yourself with them.

1 After using the quick relaxation exercise from Chapter 5, take a moment to close your eyes or let them become fuzzy and defocused.

2 Then, scan through your body. Observe the feelings in your forehead, and ask yourself: 'What am I feeling here?'

3 Then, focus on the feelings around your eyes, and ask the question again: 'What am I feeling here?' Move on to your neck and shoulders; focus on your chest, your upper and lower back, and your stomach; and then your legs. Be systematic, and remember to ask yourself at each point: 'What am I feeling here?' This whole process takes one minute.

4 It is important to *connect* with the feelings. You might detect tiredness, stress, anxiety, reluctance, anger, a desire to escape... or something else. All emotions are possible. Spend some time observing the sensations.

5 As you ask 'What am I feeling here?', thoughts will start to *pop* into your mind. Do not grasp for them; they become clear once you stop looking. Simply focus on the feelings, and let thoughts and ideas come to you.

6 As thoughts (ideas, memories, your inner voice, sudden realizations, etc.) pop into your mind, you might feel a growing intensity in your emotions. Do not suppress or judge your thoughts or feelings – connect with them, experience them, and listen to them.

7 Then, ask yourself: 'What is the problem? Why am I feeling these feelings?' Again – stay relaxed, and more ideas, memories and images will play across your mind. Observe them; don't judge, dismiss or seek to understand – and insights *will* come.

8 These thoughts will be fragments – they might make little sense and may seem unconnected or irrelevant. Go with it, and accept your ideas no matter how you feel about them. Sometimes it helps to ask questions of yourself. For example:

▷ 'What am I afraid of?'

▷ 'Why am I frustrated?'

▷ 'Why do I want to avoid this?'

▷ 'Can I see the point in doing this?'

▷ 'Am I worried about something?'

▷ 'What's the problem?'

▷ 'Why am I stressed?'

And so on... Question your stressful feelings, and you will gain insight into them.

9 *Quickly* write down the main thoughts and mental images you experience them. If your mind seems blank at first, just

relax a little. Scan through the various parts of your body, acknowledging and observing the feelings you find there. Ideas have to come. Thinking is a continual experience.

With exercises such as these, you cannot force anything. (Thinking 'I must think of something' will not help! Just concentrate on the feelings in your body, and answer the above questions.)

Remember, do not judge or censor the ideas you have – just let them come.

After a little practice, *your pen will do the writing for you* – rather than thinking about it, you'll tap into a stream of inner consciousness. By that point, you will feel connected to your emotional stresses and limitations.

10 Finally, when you feel you've expressed the potential reasons for your stress (and therefore procrastination), use the relaxation exercise once more. Breathe away the stress, frustration and anxiety you have experienced. Become calmer and more rational, and regain control. Tell yourself to 'release the emotions' you are feeling, and focus on becoming calm.

This exercise simply translates feelings into thoughts. Relax into it, connect to the sensations in your body, and let thoughts pop into your mind. Grasp around for answers, or feel cynical about this approach, and you'll just sit there thinking: 'What am I supposed to be doing?'

To avoid this, relax into your bodily feelings and pay attention when thoughts start to appear. Ask yourself: 'What is the problem? Why am I feeling these feelings?' Your answers will reflect the fear or frustration you feel. Expect these thought to be fragmented, perhaps making little sense. However, you will also gain insight. Whether you feel tired, resentful, afraid or frustrated – the beliefs *behind* those feelings will become clearer.

Often, expressing these deeper-held thoughts causes a release of pressure. People then feel relieved and subsequently more in control. At other times, you may need to see things from a different perspective – we will explore that in more detail later.

For now, practise connecting with your negative emotions, and writing down the thoughts associated with them. To see this in action, here is one of Annette's examples:

Date and time:	11 January, 6 p.m.
Activating situation:	*What task did you procrastinate about?* Writing my manuscript. *Were you finding it difficult to start a task / persevere with a task / complete a task / or get going again in between tasks?* Getting started. *Were there any noteworthy cues (location, emotional state, last action, other people)?* I was sitting at my computer - I always procrastinate there.
Belief:	*How did you excuse your decision to procrastinate. What did you say, picture or feel?* I told myself: 'I don't need to do this now - what's the point anyway?' *What negative emotions did you feel when you focused on the task?* I felt heavy, frustrated and bored. *What negative thoughts did you have about the task?* I am sick and tired of writing! It's hard, tough, I'm fed up with it. I don't even believe in it anymore. It's stupid - the whole exercise is pointless. I just want to go out and have fun. I am frustrated at having to spend so much time doing it. What's the point of doing anything when it's this hard?? I'll never get anywhere with it. I'm stupid for even trying. Stupid. Everyone knows I am.

In this example, Annette dismissed her excuses and focused on her emotions: *heavy*, *frustrated* and *bored*.

She followed the exercise above, scanning through her body while asking herself: 'What am I feeling here?' She quickly scribbled down her thoughts as they popped into her mind.

As expected, they were fragmented and not logical (or happy). However, Annette's problem is quite clear:

▶ She is 'sick and tired' of writing.

▶ She finds it tough.

▶ She doesn't believe that her project will be a success.

▶ She wants to have fun.

▶ She is frustrated at the amount of time it is taking.

▶ She feels stupid for trying to write a novel.

Bear in mind – if you had asked Annette about her writing, she would have told you (and herself): 'I love it! I finally have the time to work towards my dream!' And she would have meant it. This is the paradox of being human.

Each of us is capable of this internal contradiction. It is not that one aspect is true and the other false. Our minds are complicated, and we often find ourselves at odds with ourselves – especially regarding the challenges we encounter. Annette expressed the beliefs associated with her *negative* emotions. It is these beliefs which lead to procrastination.

Interestingly, as soon as Annette wrote down these thoughts – she felt *much* better. Having vented a little steam, her emotional perspective changed. For instance, Annette knew her work could turn out to be *really good*, but only if she worked on it; she would have to 'put the hours in'. After telling herself this, she worked happily for nine hours straight.

Focus points

✳ *It is complicated to be human; we are often caught in two minds.* You may feel positive and confident in one breath, and then anxious or frustrated in the next. Procrastination reflects the beliefs associated with our negative emotions.

✳ *Reach beyond our excuses, and we sometimes find our limiting beliefs.* They tend to be intransigent, and limited, telling us what we 'must' or 'must not' do.

* *We are not always conscious of our beliefs.* But they colour our thoughts, our perceptions, and our emotions and our behaviours.
* *It helps to understand which limiting beliefs are causing us to feel stressed.* You can gain invaluable insight into your fears and frustrations.
* *Often, pressure is released when we express our deeper-held beliefs.* We feel a sense of relief and more inclined to take action.

Putting this together

Next, you need to practise your new skills. For the next few days, focus on the following exercise. Remember – you are still learning and your efforts will not always be perfect. However, over the course of a day or two, you *will* make some progress.

As before, start by drawing up a mini-action plan.

EXERCISE: GETTING A MINI-ACTION PLAN TOGETHER

▶ This exercise takes just a minute.

▶ The aim of the exercise is to plan your next action.

▶ Use this exercise whenever you need to take action.

1 Whenever you notice yourself procrastinating, dismiss procrastination excuses using the techniques from Chapter 5. Then, ask yourself: 'What do I need to do next?'

   ▷ Is there a job that needs doing now?

   ▷ If not, select a task from your goal 'action plan'.

   ▷ Choose a task (or tasks) that you can work on for the next 15 minutes.

2 Write down the steps you will take for the next 15 minutes – no longer. Use action-oriented words, and be specific.

3 Estimate how long it will take to complete the plan (maximum: 15 minutes), and note how you'll cope

with procrastination urges. You could use the 'Dismiss procrastination excuses' exercise excuses (Chapter 5), use the quick relaxation exercise (Chapter 5), and use the 'Releasing negative emotions' exercise from this chapter.

4 Finally, identify the moments where you risk procrastination.

Completing this mini-action plan takes moments, but it tells you where to start. As you progress through your plan, tick each step when completed – or tick the whole plan when finished.

Figure 6.1 is a blank plan for you to photocopy or otherwise reproduce.

MINI-ACTION PLAN

(A) The steps I will take: _____

_____

_____

_____

(B) How long I will be active for: _____

(C) How I will cope with the urge to procrastinate: _____

_____

_____

(D) When I might get the urge to procrastinate: _____

_____

Figure 6.1 Mini-action plan

Alternatively – use your notebook, the headers looking something like this:

MINI-ACTION PLAN

STEPS:

TIME:

COPE BY:

DANGER:

When you have your mini-action plan to hand, move on to the following exercise.

EXERCISE: EXPRESSING NEGATIVE BELIEFS

> ► This exercise takes just a few minutes each time.
>
> ► The aim of the exercise it to get in touch with your negative beliefs.
>
> ► Use your notebook, or photocopied ABC records, to record the requested information.
>
> ► Carry this out multiple times over the next few *days. Complete a minimum of ten ABC records before moving on to the next chapter.*

1 Focus on the first step of your mini-action plan. You know this will take only 15 minutes to complete. How does it make you feel?

2 Then, use the quick relaxation exercise (from Chapter 5).

3 Next, scan through your body and detect any stresses or strains in your face, head, shoulders, arms, back, chest, stomach and legs. Spend a minute or so connecting with the feelings in your body.

4 Use the 'Releasing negative emotions' technique (above) to determine what you *really* believe about taking action. Sometimes your thoughts will be clear, and sometimes hazy; sometimes they will make sense, and at other times they will be irrational fragments. Avoid judging or censoring yourself. Instead, make a note of *any* ideas and thoughts as you think them.

5   As thoughts start popping into your mind, write them down. Practise a little, and you will be able to express your beliefs without even thinking about it – your fingers will do the work for you.

6   Then, use the quick relaxation exercise again and release any stress you feel. Focus on becoming calmer and more rational.

7   At this point, you might feel relieved enough to take action. You have your mini-action plan, so feel free to start. If you complete those steps, either carry on working or draw up another plan. If you start procrastinating, dismiss any excuses and use the 'Releasing negative emotions' technique once more.

Sometimes, you will find it difficult to connect with your negative thoughts and emotions. Anticipate some failure and learn from it. In the next chapter, we will practise these techniques further.

Whenever you complete the exercise above – successfully or otherwise – write up your experiences using a new ABC record. Complete ten records before moving on to Chapter 7. (It may be too much to write notes for each 15 minutes you spend working. Instead, aim for three ABC records per day.)

Figure 6.1 is the blank ABC record for you to photocopy or otherwise reproduce.

In an A5 notebook, you would want this information to take up one page:

Date and time:
Task:
Feelings:
Cues:
Excuse:
Negative beliefs:
Activity:
Pay-off:
Technique results:

Date and time:	
Activating situation:	*What task did you procrastinate about?* *Were you finding it difficult to start a task / persevere with a task / complete a task / or get going again in between tasks?* *Were there any noteworthy cues (location, emotional state, last action, other people)?*
Belief:	*How did you excuse your decision to procrastinate? What did you say, picture or feel?* *What negative emotions did you feel when you focused on the task? What negative thoughts did you have about the task?*
Consequence:	*What procrastination activity did you do (or were about to do) instead?* *How might you have found this procrastination activity rewarding?* *What happened next? Did you feel stressed or relaxed? If you felt stressed, did you understand why? Were you able to carry out your plan?*

Figure 6.2 Blank ABC record

With this exercise, you're learning to express your deeper fears and limitations. This is not easy – we shy away from our weaknesses. Do not judge or censor any thoughts that pop into your mind.

As much as possible, carry out the steps on your mini-action plan – it's just 15 minutes. Then, carry on working or draw up another. If you truly get up and running, take a 15-minute break for every hour you work.

Moving on

Expressing your negative, emotional reasoning helps to overcome procrastination. Negative beliefs are problematic because they cloud our optimism. Breaking free of that mental prison radically changes the way we do things. Here are some points to remember:

Focus points

* *On some level, we believe procrastination temporarily alleviates stress.* To an extent, this is correct.

* *Unfortunately, procrastination also causes stress.* Because we are caught between a rock and a hard place, taking action feels stressful – and procrastination feels miserable.

* *Dismissing excuses and focusing on the next 15 minutes may leave you feeling more stressed than before.* Use the quick relaxation exercise and regain your equilibrium.

* *Then, connect to your emotions and express the thoughts associated with them.* Ask yourself questions, and accept your answers without judgement or censor. Be kind to yourself.

* *Often, expressing your fears and limitations releases you from them.* You may then find it easier to act.

Next step

In this chapter you have learned a powerful technique for change. Procrastination is designed to avoid stress. You now have a better way of dealing with such feelings. Often, that will be enough.

Sometimes, our negative beliefs are too entrenched to release in this way. At such times, you need to challenge your limitations. In the next chapter, you will learn how to do that.

Changing limiting beliefs

In this chapter you will learn:

- ▶ *How beliefs are not reality and distort our thinking*
- ▶ *That limiting beliefs play a powerful role in procrastination*
- ▶ *Some typical limiting beliefs*
- ▶ *How to observe your own limiting beliefs and to move beyond them*
- ▶ *How to observe and 'spin' your negative feelings*
- ▶ *How to bring all the above techniques together as you continue to challenge your procrastination and take control.*

1 Do you fear failure?

2 Can you work only when you're in the mood?

3 Do you get frustrated because everything seems so difficult?

4 Do you give up before you've even started?

5 Does everything have to be perfect?

We are not always conscious of our beliefs, but they colour our thoughts, our feelings and our actions. Some beliefs are positive and empowering, whereas others only hold us back. They form our reality.

Beliefs can be complex and contradictory, and they become 'activated' according to our circumstances. For example, imagine you're enjoying a relaxed evening with friends. You excuse yourself to get a drink. As you walk away, you hear the group burst into laughter. You feel a sudden jolt of self-consciousness and anxiety: 'They're laughing at me! What did I do?' The chances are, they're just sharing a joke. But, in that moment, an old negative belief has been activated – and your thoughts and feelings have changed.

Our emotions are driven by our beliefs. If emotions play a part in your procrastination – and they usually do – your limiting beliefs may be holding you back.

In the previous chapter, you learned how to ease procrastination by expressing your anxieties and frustrations. Sometimes, acknowledging our negative beliefs is not enough – we must see things from a different perspective. In this chapter, you will learn how to do just that.

Did you complete the ten ABC records from Chapter 6? This chapter will make more sense when you have done so.

Decoding your thoughts

Previously, we looked at Laura's difficulties with losing weight. There were too many temptations, and she constantly excused her overeating. Overwhelmed with frustration, she would simply cave in.

Laura was taught how to express her negative beliefs at such times. Whenever temptation took hold, she scanned through her body and recorded her thoughts. Here are her answers:

▶ 'I am going to fail anyway. What's the point?'

▶ 'It's so difficult and I want to eat something! It's not fair – you're such a slave driver!'

▶ 'I hate being on a diet – it's going to go on for ever and I'll be miserable and I'll not even lose weight anyway. I'll go on holiday and I'll be fat and ugly and what's the point?'

▶ 'I might as well just give in. I just want to eat something – is that so bad?'

Noting these thoughts eased Laura's frustration slightly, but she still overate – her desire was too intense. This was her *mindset* in the moment: frustrated, pessimistic and destructive. Clearly, there are some underlying problems:

▶ '*I am going to fail anyway. What's the point?*'

   To begin, Laura is certain her diet will fail. When we strongly believe our efforts will go unrewarded, taking action becomes difficult. In Laura's case, her negative belief is borne of previous failed diets.

   Viewed rationally, Laura is capable of losing weight. If she follows her diet and exercises regularly, she will succeed. Unfortunately, this logic is overridden by her belief that failure is inevitable. In fact, her belief is causing the very failure she fears.

▶ '*It's so difficult and I want to eat something!*'

   To accomplish anything worthwhile, we must accept some frustration. On some level, Laura does not want to accept this reality. The idea that *pleasure must come first* makes her frustration intolerable.

▶ '*It's not fair – you're such a slave driver!*"

We resent following orders – including those orders we give to ourselves. Laura likes the idea of losing weight, but dieting feels like an imposition. To an extent, Laura overeats to rebel against herself.

▶ '*I hate being on a diet – it's going to go on for ever and I'll be miserable and I'll not even lose weight anyway. I'll go on holiday and I'll be fat and ugly and what's the point?*'

This statement is very pessimistic: she will fail *and* be miserable for ever. Little wonder she procrastinates about her diet. Imagine being permanently miserable, and all for nothing.

▶ '*I might as well just give in. I just want to eat something – is that so bad?*'

This is Laura's excuse to stop. It reflects her emotional viewpoint:

▷ 'I am bound to fail.'

▷ 'Dieting is difficult because pleasure should come first.'

▷ 'This diet feels like an imposition.'

▷ 'Dieting is a source of permanent misery.'

When these beliefs take hold, Laura's desire to 'give in' overwhelms her. Her strong feelings reflect the strength of her beliefs, and procrastination is inevitable.

Laura is capable of losing weight, but that truth deserts her *in the moment*. It is hard to think logically when limiting beliefs take over, and we are all prone to such moments. In fact, this is procrastination in a nutshell.

So, let's review some typical limiting beliefs behind procrastination. You will need your ABC records to hand.

Focus points

✻ *Our feelings have a basis.* Emotions are complicated and often contradictory, but they are not random experiences.

* *Writing down our thoughts when we procrastinate often helps.* However, sometimes our urge to procrastinate is too intense and we struggle to see past our limiting beliefs.
* *Emotional thinking can spiral out of control.* It becomes hard to think logically, and we become trapped by our beliefs.

Typical limiting beliefs

Read through the following list of limiting beliefs. Most of us acquire *some* of these beliefs over time. They tend to reflect childhood conclusions, drawn from difficult experiences. Later, they 'gang up' on us – becoming activated at difficult moments to create limitation and avoidance.

Consider this list of beliefs carefully; if one (or more) describes your mindset when you procrastinate, make a note of it.

EXERCISE: IDENTIFYING LIMITING BELIEFS

▶ This exercise takes 5–10 minutes.

▶ The aim is to gain greater insight into your limiting beliefs.

▶ You will need your ABC records from the previous chapter.

1 Read through the following list of negative beliefs with your ABC records to hand. Ask yourself: 'When I procrastinate, do I believe this?'

2 Sometimes you clearly will, and at other times it might just be a possibility. Keep an open mind, and consider your deeper feelings.

3 Where limiting beliefs seems familiar, check through your notes and write down relevant examples. Note down any thoughts or emotions you recognize and add any more you can think of. There will be plenty of clues in your notes.

'Pleasure must come first.'

Imagine a choice: a luxurious massage and then lunch with friends, or a dull meeting in a stuffy office. Which would you like to choose?

We have all felt torn between work and play. Focusing on our long-term interests is *difficult* when there is immediate fun to be had. For many, short-term frustration is difficult to accept.

The problem is one of 'goal conflict'. If you have an important exam to pass, you must commit to study and revision. But if you also have a busy social life, your time will be limited. Having lots of fun and passing exams are not compatible lifestyles. One will have to be sacrificed for the other, and your choice will be governed by your beliefs.

Goal conflict leads to frustration. To escape this, we resort to short-term bargaining: 'I'll make a start on this as soon as I've finished this cup of tea.' We then renege on our promises: 'OK, just one more cup of tea and then I "promise" I will make a start...'. This thinking gets out of hand, and procrastination becomes entrenched.

Life will be shallow if you constantly sacrifice your future. Significant achievement means tolerating frustration in exchange for future rewards. Of course – too much of this and life becomes impossibly dull. It is a question of balance.

Prioritizing pleasure can be symptomatic of other problems. A fear of failure or disapproval might compel us towards fun as a form of *avoidance*, even though it is not our primary desire. Limiting beliefs gang up on us; they work together, creating chronic procrastination.

Typical thoughts:

▶ 'Life is too short to be doing this.'

▶ 'I don't want to miss out!'

▶ 'I'll just enjoy this *other activity* first, and then I'll make a start.'

- 'Life is for living – it should be fun!'

- 'God, this is so boring. Let's do something else.'

Typical feelings:

- A *yearning* to do something more interesting at that moment

- Feeling frustrated at having to do something dull or routine

- A feeling that you're missing out

- Feelings of curiosity leading you away from a pressing task

'I must not fail.'

Most people fear the *idea* of failure, particularly when it involves disapproval. This is understandable; our worst experiences in life usually involve failure, especially in childhood. We quickly become averse to such a feeling – almost like a phobia. A fear of failure might cause procrastination particularly when:

- We find tasks difficult or challenging

- The outcome of a task is especially important

- We are afraid our performance will be judged.

At such times, our perception becomes distorted. Challenges are overestimated, and we can see only negative consequences. Failure is rarely fatal. In fact, it represents our best opportunity to learn. Keep your head, and such difficulties grant progress and growth. Unfortunately, we rarely see failure this way.

Instead, we lose perspective and worry how we appear to others – their opinions become too important. Beyond the fear of 'failure' resides our darkest concern: *the fear of not being good enough*. We will avoid *anything* that might confirm this.

To understand this fully, we must look to our childhood experiences. Children hate anything that might demonstrate their *inferiority*. They strive to avoid appearing weak or different, and then carry this habit into adulthood. Left unchecked, this anxiety causes chronic procrastination.

There is an emotional logic to this. Who wants to experience the pain of failure, disapproval and rejection?

This is not a rational matter but a visceral experience. Logically, we know delay will only increase our chances of failure. However – procrastination is driven by emotions, not reason. And if we *do* fail, we can tell ourselves: 'Well, OK, but it doesn't matter because I didn't really try.' Is this a familiar thought? This is a trap. It leads only to disappointment.

Perhaps surprisingly, we can fear failure despite feeling confident in our abilities. Here, our natural confidence is overridden; the general fear of failure distorts our perceptions. Over time, procrastination becomes habitual and even simple tasks are needlessly delayed.

Typical thoughts:

▶ 'I must get this right.'

▶ 'It's not good enough – it's ruined.'

▶ 'Oh God, they'll think I'm stupid.'

▶ 'I'm going to mess this up.'

▶ 'Nobody else can ever see this.'

▶ 'I could have done it, but I didn't try.'

▶ 'I know I'm going to fail.'

Typical feelings:

▶ Fear and anxiety

▶ A strong feeling of resistance when trying to take action

▶ A sense of pessimism, like something bad is going to happen

'I must not succeed.'

That people fear success might seem strange, but it is a common cause of procrastination:

We might progress faster than our peers or family, causing a rift, jealousy or unwanted attention.

It could lead to additional expectation and responsibility. In this case, the fear of success is a fear of *eventual* failure.

Typical thoughts:

▶ 'I don't want to do this.'

▶ 'I'm worried what people will think.'

▶ 'Doing this will just make everything worse.'

Typical feelings:

▶ Fear and anxiety

▶ A strong feeling of resistance when trying to take action.

▶ A sense of pessimism, like something bad is going to happen.

'Things must not change.'

Many people fear the unknown. As a result they crave security. Change might bring difficulty and complication, whereas inaction is a safer bet. 'If nothing changes, then at least nothing bad can happen!' This fear reflects a deep pessimism and leads to profound inertia. Even the smallest action can be rejected.

Have you ever walked past a dirty plate and decided to ignore it? Needlessly *refusing* to act may indicate an entrenched, irrational need for things to stay the same. Unfortunately, this inertia causes significant difficulties in life.

Typical thoughts:

▶ 'Let's just do that later.'

▶ 'I need to prepare properly – what if it all goes wrong?'

▶ 'Something bad is going to happen, I can feel it.'

▶ 'If I solve this problem, something bad is bound to happen.'

▶ 'It's not worth the risk.'

▶ 'This could turn out really bad.'

▶ 'Let's just leave it for now.'

Typical feelings:

- Fear and anxiety
- A strong feeling of resistance when trying to take action
- A yearning for things to stay the same
- A sense of pessimism, as if something bad is going to happen

'It has to be perfect.'

Nobody likes to fail. For some, this means striving for *perfection* – an overcompensation that causes stress and anxiety. Deep down, we know perfection is unattainable. We then feel unconfident and discouraged before we even start. Naturally, we then procrastinate.

Perfectionism also leads to over-preparation. Although this *can* be helpful (attention to detail is the difference between being very good and excellent), it often gets in the way. Many tasks require a 'rough and ready' approach to start, with refinement coming later. If you agonize over every detail, you'll waste a considerable amount of time. 'Perfect planning' is also a form of procrastination.

Perfectionism distorts our decision-making. As we approach the end of a task, we might wish to tear it all up and start again. Deep down, we fear imperfection might bring unwanted attention. This makes no logical sense, but perfectionism is another strategy to avoid the pain of failure, rejection and being exposed as 'not good enough'.

Typical thoughts

- 'It has to be better.'
- 'I need to get this right.'
- 'This is terrible – I need to start from scratch.'
- 'Why is it not good enough?'
- 'I don't want to do it.'
- 'I might as well just give up.'

Typical feelings:

▶ A strong sense of anxiety

▶ A strong feeling of resistance when trying to take action

▶ A yearning to do something less stressful

▶ A strong feeling of disappointment

▶ A desire to start again from scratch

We have covered the first five limiting beliefs that cause procrastination. We will add to this list later. Before that, let's explore the pernicious effect these beliefs have on the human mind.

!

Focus points

✳ *Pleasure must come first.* This belief is a strategy for avoiding unpleasant feelings. It is problematic because life is generally frustrating, especially when working towards our goals.

✳ *I must not fail.* A key limiting belief, encompassing the fear of judgement, rejection and being found out as 'not good enough'. At its worst, this belief becomes an entrenched habit leading to chronic procrastination.

✳ *I must not succeed.* Perhaps surprisingly, many people fear success. It could lead to unwanted attention or separation, or perhaps additional responsibility. We procrastinate to avoid these circumstances.

✳ *Things must not change.* We often crave security. Change might bring difficulty, whereas inaction keeps us safe. This reflects a deeply held pessimism, and can cause us to procrastinate about anything.

✳ *It has to be perfect.* Achievement is gradual, but perfectionism does not reflect this. Instead, we 'perfectly plan' action, or lack confidence in our efforts. Perfectionism is a fear-based strategy to avoid failure, rejection and being 'not good enough'.

Beliefs are not reality

Our limiting beliefs are not rational, although they can contain some truth. Typically, they are just *generalizations*; they rarely stand up to logic or reason. However, our beliefs define our reality. Positive beliefs are motivating, but limiting beliefs create frustration and fear.

Beneficial or otherwise, we make our beliefs *real*. This isn't a conscious or rational process. In difficult moments, limiting beliefs dominate our mindset; our thoughts, feelings and behaviours all change. Later, when the moment has passed, we're left wondering: 'Why did I just do that?'

A perfect example of this can be found when dieting. After some moderate progress, things start to slip. Subtle, unconscious and self-sabotaging behaviours creep in. Eventually, the weight is regained. Continued weight loss would have challenged certain beliefs (e.g. 'I cannot lose weight'). Instead, the status quo is maintained.

You have two choices: strive against your limiting beliefs, or conform to them. They are your *familiar* reality, and unless you re-educate your emotional understanding – you will always struggle with procrastination.

Further limiting beliefs

Let's continue with our list of beliefs. As before, have your ABC records to hand. If a limiting belief is familiar, check through your notes and write down one or two examples. Make a note of any thoughts or emotions you recognize.

'I hate being told what to do.'

We tend to resent other people's instructions or 'advice'. From an early age, there has been a queue of people waiting to lay down the law: your parents, your teachers, lecturers and bosses, perhaps your friends, or even your partner...

As adults, when told *what* to do (or *how* to do it), we can feel angry and powerless. Procrastination becomes a way of reasserting control or gaining revenge. Wilfulness takes over, and the task is delayed or put from our mind – even to our own detriment.

Typical thoughts:

▶ 'Why do I have to do this?'

▶ 'This is pointless.'

- ▶ 'I shouldn't have to this just because I've been told.'

- ▶ 'I shouldn't have to do things I don't want to do.'

- ▶ 'I'll show them, I'm just not doing it.'

- ▶ 'I *hate* being told what to do!'

Typical feelings:

- ▶ A strong sense of resentment

- ▶ A strong feeling of resistance when trying to take action

- ▶ A yearning to abandon the task, to send a message

'I have plenty of time' and 'I work best under pressure.'

Some people genuinely believe they work best under pressure. And usually, there is some truth to this belief. At first, we feel complacent – distant deadlines are ignored, and we focus on more rewarding activities.

As deadlines approach, the consequences of our inaction become clearer. Pressure then motivates us, and we make a start – albeit often too late. This approach causes significant problems. Leaving everything to the last minute is stressful and leaves little time for when things go wrong – as they often do. Missed deadlines become normal, and we perform below our best. Rather than achieving something special, at best we end up with something 'good enough'.

Sometimes, this suits our needs; we have avoided doing our very best, so now there is a get-out clause: 'I could have achieved more if I'd spent more time on it.' Once more, this protects us from failure, disapproval and rejection.

Time is our most precious resource. We know this intellectually, but it slips from our grasp all too easily. The fallacy of having *too much time* is the most irrational, limiting belief on this list.

Typical thoughts:

- ▶ 'I don't need to do this yet.'

- ▶ 'It's OK to leave this.'

- ▶ 'I work best under pressure.'
- ▶ 'I'll get this sorted before I need to.'

Typical feelings:

- ▶ A sense of complacency when procrastinating
- ▶ A strong feeling of urgency when tasks finally have to be done

'It's too difficult' and 'I cannot do it.'

The fear of failure is a *generalized* belief – we are discouraged, even when confident in our ability. The negative consequences of failing appear so tremendous, our confidence gives way to fear. We know we are capable, but delay anyway.

The limiting beliefs 'I cannot do it' and 'It's too difficult' are subtly different. Instead, we worry our abilities will fail us, which then causes significant problems. We may overestimate the challenges involved, or even give up entirely and hope somebody else will take over. This erodes our self-respect, and we lose the opportunity to learn.

We only truly master something via repetition; everyone has to start somewhere. Instead, poor confidence defeats us from the outset. Procrastination halts our progress and becomes entrenched.

A variation on this theme is the idea of 'being unworthy'. Our poor self-belief is compounded by an unforgiving attitude, and we judge ourselves in the harshest possible terms. These limiting beliefs drive us towards self-sabotage and neglect.

Typical thoughts:

- ▶ 'It's too hard.'
- ▶ 'I can't do it.'
- ▶ 'I'm no good at this.'
- ▶ 'I don't have enough willpower.'

- 'I don't deserve this.'
- 'If I know I can't do it – why bother starting?'
- 'Everyone will know I'm useless.'

Typical feelings:

- A strong sense of anxiety and frustration
- A strong feeling of resistance when trying to take action
- A feeling that we're about to make a fool of ourselves
- A yearning to avoid the task

'It shouldn't be this hard. Why do I have to keep doing it?'

You cannot become fit and healthy via one epic gym session. You need to build it up steadily, for a period of months, before gains will be made. The simple truth is: achieving anything takes sustained effort, and many baulk at the challenge.

All procrastination involves abandoning our best interests. Many people feel they have little choice because taking action feels so uncomfortable. We are drawn to the easier route, even though it will cause future stress and difficulty. But our logical understanding is overridden by an intolerance of frustration and discomfort.

Combine this intolerance with wishful thinking, and we then procrastinate. Learning to tolerate frustration is *key*. This capacity can only be developed with practice. In later chapters, we will look at specific techniques to help.

Typical thoughts:

- 'It's too hard!'
- 'I can't do it!'
- 'I'm too stressed.'
- 'I've already done this once!'
- 'I shouldn't have to keep doing this.'
- 'Let's do something easier.'

- ‘What is the point?’
- ‘Let’s just stop for a bit.’

Typical feelings:

- A strong sense of anxiety, frustration and even emotional pain
- A strong feeling of resistance when trying to take action
- A yearning to avoid the task

‘I’m too tired’, ‘I’m too stressed’ and ‘I’m not in the mood!’

As mentioned earlier, taking action can be frustrating – particularly when negative beliefs hold sway. Hard work becomes *even more difficult* when we feel stressed, tired or pessimistic.

We are much more likely to procrastinate when we’re ‘not in the mood’. Negative feelings interfere with our judgement; we overestimate the effort required and lose sight of our capabilities. Many people cite tiredness, hunger or stress as a reason for procrastination.

Stress and tiredness increase the power of other negative beliefs, making procrastination even more likely. Even when tired or stressed, we *could* take action if we needed to. But this reality is lost in our desire to stop and rest. Tiredness becomes our excuse.

Typical thoughts:

- ‘I’m too tired.’
- ‘I’m too stressed.’
- ‘I’m too anxious.’
- ‘I work better when I’m fresh.’

Typical feelings:

- A strong sense of frustration
- A strong feeling that there is no point starting yet
- A desire to delay or abandon the task

'I can't work like this.'

Similar to 'I'm too tired', imperfect circumstances give us a perfect 'reason' to procrastinate. We might not have *enough time* to make an impact. It may be *too noisy*, or *too warm*, or *too cold*. We might not have *everything we need*, or it might be *too messy to concentrate*. It might be *better to start after the weekend*. And so on...

And yet, in most circumstances, we could start right now – if we *really* had to. Things may never be just right. We are taking the unfavourable, and using it as an excuse.

Typical thoughts

▶ 'I've not got enough time to start now.'

▶ 'I've not got everything I need.'

▶ 'I need to take care of this before I start.'

▶ 'There is no point starting this now.'

▶ 'It's too noisy/quiet/cold/warm, etc.'

▶ 'I need to wait until things are right.'

▶ 'I can't work like this.'

▶ 'I'll start tomorrow / after the weekend / after my birthday / etc.'

▶ 'Let's just wait until conditions are more suitable.'

Typical feelings:

▶ A strong sense of lethargy

▶ A strong feeling of resistance when trying to take action

▶ A desire to sort out a pressing problem other than the task you're procrastinating over

▶ A yearning to wait until circumstances are more conducive

Procrastination is caused by countless limiting beliefs – these are just the most common. As you read through this list, which did you identify with? When you procrastinate, some of these beliefs will dominate your mindset. Learning to recognize them will be of great benefit.

So, let's explore two techniques to transform negative beliefs.

Focus points

* *I hate being told what to do.* Most of us dislike following orders, and procrastination becomes a way of reasserting control or gaining revenge.
* *I have plenty of time, and I work best under pressure.* Distant deadlines leave us feeling complacent, so we focus on more rewarding things. We are motivated by pressure when deadlines approach, but it's often too late to do our best.
* *It's too difficult, and I cannot do it.* When we worry our abilities will fail us, we overestimate the challenges involved. We may even give up entirely, in the hope that somebody else will take over.
* *It shouldn't be this hard. Why do I have to keep doing it?* To achieve anything worthwhile, we have to make a sustained effort. For many, this is too frustrating to bear.
* *I'm too tired, I'm too stressed, and I'm not in the mood!* Tiredness is a major cause of procrastination. Stress, tiredness and pessimism change our relationship with *effort*, and we allow ourselves to give up.
* *I can't work like this.* Imperfect circumstances give us a reason to procrastinate. We might not have enough time, or it could be too noisy, or too warm; there are numerous excuses available – all of which lead to procrastination.

Thinking rationally

Limiting beliefs distort our thinking, and procrastination seems like the only option. At such times, restoring rational thought is key. When negative beliefs hold sway over our perception, choice is lost to us. By reconnecting to a logical viewpoint in the moment, we are free to *choose* our next action.

EXERCISE: RATIONAL AFFIRMATIONS

▶ This exercise takes just a few seconds each time.

▶ The aim is to step beyond limiting beliefs and think rationally.

▶ Use this technique whenever you find yourself procrastinating.

1 Whenever you feel unable to take positive action, complete the 'Releasing negative emotions' exercise from the previous chapter. Get in touch with stressful feelings and write down the associated negative thoughts.

2 Then, take a moment to relax and state the following affirmations to yourself. Use the 'certain inner voice' which you practised in Chapter 5:

  ▷ By *doing this now*, I am becoming healthier/happier/more successful/stronger/more confident, etc.
  ▷ By *doing this now*, I am overcoming my fear of *something*.

3 Then, make a start – even just for the 15 minutes.

Every action – or inaction – counts towards something; our lives are enriched or impoverished by the decisions we make. This affirmation empowers you because it is the *truth*. Even strong negative beliefs cannot override this logic. Consider these examples:

▶ By starting this report, I am becoming more successful in my job.

▶ By cleaning the kitchen, I am becoming happier with my living space.

▶ By making this phone call, I am overcoming my fear of being shouted at.

▶ By writing my essay now, I am overcoming my fear of disapproval.

▶ By running these errands now, I am becoming more organized.

▶ By exercising now, I am becoming healthier and stronger.

Although simple, this exercise is incredibly powerful. You cannot labour under a negative belief *and* think logically at the same time. These affirmations are indisputable. With practice, limiting beliefs become meaningless.

Remember to identify the *true benefit* of taking action. When that is clear in your mind, you will gain greater control of your thoughts and actions.

Working with feelings

As we have learned, there is a strong connection between our thoughts and emotions. When negative beliefs take over, we tend to feel difficult feelings. In the previous chapter, you learned how to alleviate such feelings by expressing your fears and frustrations. Although often effective, sometimes you need a more direct approach.

This next exercise harnesses your imagination to control your emotions. This will take a little practice, but keep an open mind and you'll soon master it. This exercise works best when preceded by the 'Quick relaxation' exercise from Chapter 5. Here it is again:

EXERCISE: THE QUICK RELAXATION EXERCISE

▶ This exercise takes just a few moments.

▶ The aim is to use slow breathing and affirmations to relax your physiology.

▶ Use this technique many times over the next few days, and particularly whenever you are procrastinating.

1 To begin, breathe in slowly through your nose, mentally counting to 5 as you do so.

2 Then, slowly exhale through your mouth, relaxing your shoulders as you breathe out.

3 Repeat this three times. When you exhale, relax your shoulders, jaw, back, stomach and feet. These areas of the body often carry tension.

4 As you exhale, tell yourself: 'I'm becoming focused and rational.'

Changing difficult emotion can make a tremendous difference to our lives. Perhaps we should be taught this as children. The following exercise may at first seem a little abstract, but persevere – it is a powerful technique.

EXERCISE: SPINNING NEGATIVE FEELINGS

▶ This exercise takes five minutes; practise it often.

▶ The aim is to learn how to change your feelings.

▶ When you get the hang of this exercise, you'll realize it is very simple.

▶ Read through the steps first and familiarize yourself with them.

Part 1: Observing negative feelings

Spend a fair amount of time answering these questions. For some, this will be really easy. For others, it will take a little time.

1 Think about a task you normally procrastinate over: something challenging and difficult. In a moment, close your eyes and imagine starting it now. Picture it in your mind, making it vivid and bright, so it feels as if you're there. Suspend your disbelief, as if you are an actor in a film.

2 Imagine this vividly enough, and you will start to feel negative emotions – particularly in your stomach or chest. Imagine hating the task, and really wanting to procrastinate. Then, ask yourself: 'What is happening in my body?'

3 Focus on the emotion you feel. Is it anxiety? Resistance? Pessimism? Frustration? Something else? Spend some of time connecting with the emotion, and answer the following questions in your notebook:

   ▷ Where is the feeling in my body (stomach, chest, face, cheeks, shoulders, etc.)?

   ▷ How does the feeling move? Is it a rising feeling or a sinking feeling? Is it a tight knot, spinning clockwise or anticlockwise?

▷ Does the feeling move quickly or slowly?

▷ What texture does the feeling have? Smooth, fuzzy, rough, tingly, spiky or texture-*less*?

▷ Is the feeling narrow or wide? Is it hotter or colder than the rest of my body?

▷ How intense is the feeling, on a scale of 1–10? Does it generate pressure, or is the feeling light?

▷ If the feeling had a colour, what would it be? (It is OK to guess!)

4 In this part of the exercise, you are recreating the feelings you get when you procrastinate. They may feel weaker than in 'real-life'. Run through it several times to answer these questions.

5 Notice how feelings move through your body, as if creating a circuit. When determining *how* they move, it helps to use your hands – as if you were showing somebody else. For example:

▷ Feelings can spin quickly in your stomach or chest (a tight feeling).

▷ They can move from your stomach, through your chest, and into your shoulders and throat (a rising feeling).

▷ They can move down from your chest and into your stomach (a sinking feeling).

▷ They can be in your torso, your legs, the top of your head, your shoulders or arms...

And so on... There are *many* possibilities – your feelings are unique to you.

6 Repeat Part 1 several times. Get a clear overview of how it feels to procrastinate.

Part 2: Spinning negative feelings

The second part of this exercise is straightforward. You're going to learn how to ease negative feelings away by 'spinning' them backwards.

Imagine sitting in a bath, scooping up handfuls of water and creating waves. Then, imagine you could reach into your procrastination feelings and do the same thing – also creating waves.

In Part 1 of the exercise, you observed how these feelings moved through your body. Next, you're going to learn how to create waves in the feeling, so they flow *backwards*. So, if your procrastinating urge moved *upwards*, from stomach to chest, you'd aim to push those feelings down, so they move in the opposite direction – from your chest into your stomach.

▶ Link the movement you're trying to create with your breathing. Imagine creating waves in the emotion (moving them backwards) each time you exhale.

▶ For some, it helps to visualize a feather duster or waterfall pushing the feelings away.

▶ Many people find the 'waves in a bath' metaphor effective.

▶ Others may prefer to spin the feelings, so move in the opposite direction, simply using their imagination.

It does not matter which method you choose – find your own way of doing this. As well as pushing the feelings backwards, practise reducing their texture, width, speed and intensity:

▶ If the feeling is tingly, imagine it becoming softer.

▶ If the feeling is wide, imagine it becoming narrower.

▶ If you gave the feeling a red colour, imagine it becoming pink, and then white or grey...

It is easier to experience than read about. Go through each step first and familiarize yourself with the process.

1 In a moment, close your eyes and imagine the procrastination scenario once more. Make it clear in your mind, suspend your disbelief and imagine you're there right now. Observe the location, movement, texture, width and intensity of the feeling (as in Part 1 of the exercise).

If a particular negative belief causes you problems, express it now and run those thoughts through your mind. For a moment, get in touch with your fear and limitation (to *some* extent – don't let it become overwhelming!)

2 Then, take a deep breath and exhale, while imagining brushing/easing/spinning the negative feeling backwards – so it moves in the opposite direction. Continue to breathe deeply, and move the feeling backwards.

It takes just a little practice to use your imagination in this way. When you get the hang of it, you'll have a 'eureka!' moment.

3 Continue spinning the feelings backwards while thinking about procrastinating:

▷ Keep the feeling moving backwards.

▷ Imagine the feeling growing narrower and less intense.

▷ What colour did you give the feeling? Make it fade, so it becomes weaker.

4 Continue with this for a minute or two. The emotions will wax and wane, which is to be expected. Sometimes, you'll need to refocus on the scenario and bring the negative feeling back.

5 After a while, one of two things will happen:

a The negative emotions will lessen to the point of vanishing, even as you vividly imagine procrastinating.

b The negative feeling will become its opposite, leading to a feeling of *motivation*.

Feelings rise and fall in intensity, and this exercise requires some practice. Once you get the hang of it, you will quickly see its usefulness. Aim to change emotions in all ways possible:

▶ Make them less 'textured'.

▶ Make them narrower and shallower.

▶ Make them slow down, and become less intense.

▶ Make them change direction, so they flow 'backwards'.

Master this, and you will change your relationship with procrastination. To practise, use it *whenever* you experience difficult feelings in day-to-day life, and especially when procrastination strikes.

Putting this together

As always, you need to practise your new skills. For the next few days, pay attention to procrastination excuses and activities, and also to your emotions. Look at your goal worksheet and action plan, and work out what you need to do next. Start by getting a mini-action plan together.

EXERCISE: GETTING A MINI-ACTION PLAN TOGETHER

▶ This exercise takes just a minute.

▶ The aim of the exercise it to plan your next action

▶ Use this exercise whenever you need to take action.

1 As always, start by asking yourself: 'What do I need to do next?'

   ▷ Is there a job that needs doing now?

   ▷ If not, select a task from your goal 'action plan'.

   ▷ Choose a task (or tasks) that you can work on for the next 30 minutes.

2 Write down the steps you will take for the next 30 minutes – no longer. Use action-oriented words, and be specific.

3 Estimate how long it will take to complete the plan (maximum: 30 minutes), and note how you'll cope with procrastination urges. You could dismiss procrastination excuses, use the quick relaxation exercise, and use the 'Rational affirmations' and 'Spinning negative emotions' techniques from this chapter.

4 Finally, write down the moments where you risk procrastination.

Get used to drawing up mini-action plans – they are invaluable. Remember to break steps down into smaller chunks if required.

Figure 7.1 is a blank plan for you to photocopy or otherwise reproduce:

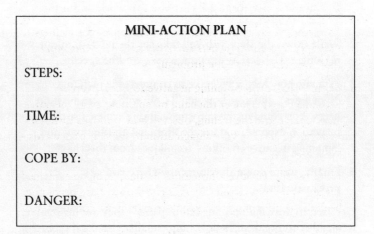

MINI-ACTION PLAN

(A) The steps I will take: _____

_____

_____

(B) How long I will be active for: _____

(C) How I will cope with the urge to procrastinate: _____

_____

_____

(D) When I might get the urge to procrastinate: _____

_____

_____

Figure 7.1 Blank mini-action plan

Alternatively, use your notebook, the headers looking something like this:

MINI-ACTION PLAN

STEPS:

TIME:

COPE BY:

DANGER:

When you have your mini-action plan to hand, move on to the following exercise.

EXERCISE: TRANSCENDING NEGATIVE BELIEFS

▶ This exercise takes just a few minutes each time.

▶ The aim of the exercise it to step beyond limiting beliefs and take action.

▶ Use your notebook, or photocopied ABC records, to record the requested information.

▶ Carry this out multiple times over the next few days. Complete a minimum of ten ABC records before moving on to the next chapter.

1 Whenever you find yourself procrastinating, dismiss any procrastination excuses, and consider the task at hand. Check your goal worksheet and action plan regularly.

2 Then, draw up a mini-action plan as directed above.

3 Next, use the relaxation exercise (found earlier in this chapter) – take a moment and *relax*.

4 How do you feel? Scan through your body and detect the feelings in your face, head, shoulders, arms, back, chest, stomach and legs. Spend a minute or so connecting with your emotions.

5 Use the technique, practised in the previous chapter, to write down the thoughts and ideas associated with your feelings. *Identify any limiting beliefs currently active in your mind.* Ask yourself: 'What's the problem?'

6 Then, practise the 'Spinning negative feelings' exercise (explained earlier). Get the hang of 'spinning away' negative emotions: locate the feeling, observe how it moves through your body, and use your imagination to move it backwards – until it changes.

7 Next, use the 'Positive affirmations' technique, again explained earlier. State to yourself, 'By *doing this now*, I am becoming healthier/happier/more successful/stronger/more confident, etc.'

Note: when combined, these two exercises are *very* powerful.

8 Then, carry out the steps on your mini-action plan. If excuses pop into your mind, dismiss them and *act*.

9 When you have finished the 30 minutes (or completed the task), make some brief notes on the experience. Do not skip this – see below for more information.

Complete these steps, and you should overcome your urge to procrastinate – at least on some occasions. If you struggle, repeat the process and try again. When your 30 minutes are complete, take a quick 15-minute break, and draw up a new plan for the next 30 minutes.

With practice, the exercises in this chapter should help. If you don't seem to get anywhere – don't panic! We'll explore further techniques in the next chapters.

Whenever you complete this exercise, successfully or otherwise, write up your experiences using a new ABC record. Complete ten records before moving on to Chapter 8. Note: you do not need to write notes for each 30 minutes of work you complete. Aim for three ABC records each day.

Figure 7.2 is the blank ABC record for you to photocopy or otherwise reproduce.

In an A5 notebook, you would want this information to take up one page:

Date and time:

Task:

Feelings:

Cues:

Excuse:

Negative beliefs:

Activity:

Pay-off:

Technique results:

Affirmation:

Date and time:	
Activating situation:	*What task did you procrastinate about?* *Were you finding it difficult to start a task / persevere with a task / complete a task / or get going again in between tasks?* *Were there any noteworthy cues (location, emotional state, last action, other people)?*
Belief:	*How did you excuse your decision to procrastinate. What did you say, picture or feel?* *What negative emotions did you feel when you focused on the task?* *What negative thoughts did you have about the task?*
Consequence:	*What procrastination activity did you do (or were you about to do) instead?* *How might you have found this procrastination activity rewarding?* *What happened next? Did you feel stressed or relaxed? If you felt stressed, did you understand why? Were you able to carry out your plan?* *What affirmation did you use? Were you able to 'spin' the feelings?*

Figure 7.2 Blank ABC record

Practise this exercise ten times over the next few days. It is very straightforward; you're building on your work from the previous chapter, and using the spinning feelings/positive affirmation technique.

Quick fix: Disprove your negative thoughts

Whenever you tell yourself, 'By doing this now, I am becoming healthier/ happier, etc.', remember to check, after taking action, whether your positive affirmation did state the *truth*.

For example, if you tell yourself, 'By cleaning the kitchen now, I am becoming happier with my living environment,' take a moment to survey your work and ask yourself: 'OK – am I happier with it now, compared to how it was?' Overcoming negative beliefs means disproving them. Remember to acknowledge your achievements – no matter how small.

Do your best to master this process, and attempt 30 minutes of action where possible. The only way to change is by *taking action*. If you manage 30 minutes, take a 15-minute break before starting the next.

Moving on

In this chapter, you have learned about limiting beliefs and explored exercises that help. Practise them thoroughly, and you will make good progress. In the meantime, bear the following points in mind:

Focus points

✳ *At certain moments, negative beliefs dominate our mindset.* We then lose focus and procrastinate.

✳ *Paying more attention to your thoughts,* particularly when you are procrastinating, will help to identify the negative beliefs at play.

✳ *Beliefs are just ideas held with conviction.* No matter how powerful they feel, beliefs are not real.

✳ *You can dispel negative beliefs by forcing yourself to think truthfully.* Practise the 'Rational affirmations' exercise in this chapter, and you will change your limiting beliefs.

✳ *There is a strong link between our thoughts and feelings.* Use the 'Spinning negative feelings' exercise to remove (or at least weaken) negative emotions, and procrastination will be easier to overcome.

Next step

Next, we will explore the relationship between effort and reward – two key factors in building motivation. For now, practise the exercises learned so far.

Effort and reward

In this chapter you will learn:

- ► *How to optimize your motivation*
- ► *The effort: reward ratio and its relationship with procrastination*
- ► *How to effort, enjoyment and reward*
- ► *How to value even delayed reward*
- ► *How to use the 'Contrasting' technique to understand the need for change*
- ► *How to reward yourself*
- ► *How to bring all the above techniques together as you continue to challenge your procrastination and take control.*

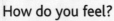

How do you feel?

1 Do you often miss deadlines?

2 Do you wonder why you can't get going?

3 Do you fail to see the value in taking action?

4 Do your efforts often go unrewarded?

5 Are you discouraged by a lack of motivation?

We procrastinate more when tasks are *viewed* as difficult or pointless. In this chapter, you will learn how to optimize your motivation. First, let's review your progress so far.

Read through the following list of techniques, and tick those you have made progress with. Take your time, and be honest with yourself.

I have practised the following exercises, and can apply them when required:

Chapter 3:

❏ Recognize procrastination types: *denial*, *refusal* and *delay*.

❏ Identify activating situations when they occur.

Chapter 4:

❏ Identify important cues which lead to procrastination.

❏ Identify procrastination excuses, activities and rewards.

Chapter 5:

❏ Use the quick relaxation exercise.

❏ Dismiss verbal and visual procrastination excuses.

❏ Draw up quick mini-action plans.

Chapter 6:

❏ Express thoughts associated with stressful emotions.

Chapter 7:

❑ Identify limiting beliefs when I procrastinate.

❑ Use the 'Spinning negative feelings' exercise to weaken negative emotions.

❑ Use the 'Rational affirmations' exercise to focus on reality.

We have covered a lot of ground so far, and there is a lot to take in. Do you think you have made solid progress, or are your skills a little patchy? If there are no gaps – well done, you are ready to build on your success. If you've not practised as much as you'd like, reread the appropriate chapter(s). There is no point in racing ahead.

In the meantime, consider the following *challenge*.

Effort versus reward

You are offered £10,000 to climb a steep, scrubby hill. It's a hot day, there is no path to speak of, and it really is steep. It will take at least a couple of hours, perhaps longer. However, your reward awaits you – should you make it to the top.

It's a stiff challenge, but £10,000 is a lot of money. How would you spend it? Is it worth the effort? Would you accept the challenge? Understandably, many people would. So, let's change things slightly.

Imagine the same steep hill on the same hot day. This time, to earn your £10,000 you must climb this hill twice per day – for the *next 100 days*. Do you still feel motivated? Probably less than before.

Finally, you're now offered just £5 to repeatedly climb this hill. To most, this will seem laughably unappealing. There is no reason to accept this challenge. It is pointless!

Why does our motivation change? The answer is found in the ratio between the *effort* we must expend, and our *valuation* of the rewards we hope to receive.

- The first example is worthwhile: the ratio between effort and reward is attractive, and we feel motivated.

- In the second example, although the reward is valuable, the effort is too much.

- In the third example, your efforts would be poorly rewarded. There is little point in accepting this challenge.

Valuable rewards build motivation, depending on the effort required. By adjusting our perception of this ratio, we can increase or decrease motivation accordingly.

ENJOYMENT MITIGATES EFFORT

Let's return to our original challenge, only this time it's posed to somebody who *loves* hill-running. Naturally, they would accept. The reward is valuable, and the activity is enjoyable. For our hill runner this is a win-win situation.

They may still accept for even just £5. It is an activity they love, and their enjoyment mitigates the effort it will take. The run itself is inherently rewarding.

Similarly, motivation changes when we dislike a task. You may know somebody who would flatly refuse to even *think* about running up a hill – no matter how great the reward. Their distaste for the activity heightens the effort required, and the challenge is rejected without consideration.

What does all of this show us?

- Increase (or decrease) the reward, and our motivation changes accordingly.

- Change the perceived effort required, and again our motivation changes.

- Action takes *less* effort when we enjoy it; tasks become inherently rewarding.

- Action takes *more* effort when we dislike it. We lose sight of the rewards we might gain.

- Adjusting your mindset changes your relationship with motivation, and therefore procrastination.

BALANCING EFFORT, ENJOYMENT AND REWARD

Effort is a subjective experience; for example, cleaning is therapeutic for some and a chore for others. Procrastination is affected by effort. We rarely delay enjoyable activities. Instead, we struggle where tasks seem frustrating, anxiety-provoking, onerous or dull. This is something we can change – perceptions are not set in stone.

Worthwhile activity is the key to a fulfilling life. Without it, you will always feel stuck. Learn to motivate yourself, and life improves in many ways:

▶ You avoid the *frustration* of procrastination.

▶ You avoid the *disappointment* of missing out.

▶ You avoid the *stress* of future complications.

▶ You earn the *satisfaction* of getting things done.

▶ You experience *rewards* in life: e.g. acceptance, status, accomplishment, financial security, acknowledgement, money, control, competence, material possessions, etc.

It is time to ingrain these truths into your mindset. The affirmations from the previous chapter help. For example:

▶ By *doing this now*, I am avoiding the frustration of procrastination.

▶ By *doing this now*, I am avoiding the stress of future problems.

▶ By *doing this now*, I am experiencing the satisfaction of getting things done.

▶ By *doing this now*, I am achieving greater status / earning more money / improving my competence, etc.

Use these affirmations regularly, and you will learn a fundamental lesson: 'Life is more enjoyable when you live it, rather than delaying it!'

Focus points

✷ *When action requires considerable effort, it is difficult to feel motivated;* particularly where it leads to little or no reward.

- ✻ *We feel more motivated when we reduce the effort required,* even if we do not value the reward.
- ✻ *We feel very motivated when we mitigate the effort* (as above), and value the rewards we will receive.

The relationship between effort and reward explains the *persistence* of procrastination. It requires little effort, it can be enjoyable, and – to our brains at least – it seems rewarding because procrastination relieves stress, albeit temporarily.

Instead, you can train yourself to *value* positive action. Motivation improves, particularly when you decrease the effort required to act. This approach is very reliable; it is difficult to feel motivated *and* procrastinate at the same time.

DELAYED REWARDS

Let's go back to our steep, scrubby hill. Again, you're offered the challenge: climb up the hill and receive £10,000. Only this time, you have to wait for five years before receiving your reward.

This proposition feels much less attractive. Motivation decreases significantly when rewards are delayed. To our brain, delayed rewards are not real. Instead, we find it easier to focus on immediate matters.

How does this relate to procrastination? Consider these examples:

▶ There is a project to complete, but the deadline is months away. Even though you should make a start, you procrastinate. Having fun now provides immediate value. Working on the project does not – it feels much less attractive in comparison.

▶ People often struggle when dieting. Losing weight might bring confidence, but this future reward feels less important when compared to the pleasure of eating now.

▶ A young musician wishes to improve their technique, but the reward of mastering their instrument seems distant when compared to relaxing with friends. The latter is instantly rewarding.

Sacrificing immediate pleasure for distant rewards is *frustrating*! Unless we concentrate, delayed rewards lose their value, and acting towards them *seems* to take more effort. In this respect, we are hardwired to procrastinate.

When evaluating possible rewards, there is another important factor to consider. And it can profoundly alter our motivation.

EXPECTANCY OF SUCCESS

One last time, let's revisit our hill and the £10,000. You're offered the same challenge, except the reward is not guaranteed. In fact, the odds are evenly matched. Although some people may retain their motivation, many will be reluctant to gamble.

The value we place on a reward depends on our *chances* of receiving it. If you were 90 per cent certain to receive the £10,000, your motivation would diminish slightly. Reduce the likelihood to 10 per cent, and motivation falls away dramatically. In this case, external factors have altered your *expectancy*. Because it is uncertain, the rewards have less value and you lose motivation.

Internal factors – such as our limiting beliefs – also modify expectancy. Believe failure is inevitable, and you will feel less inclined to act. Your low expectations have weakened your motivation.

Again, you can see how it relates to procrastination:

▷ You have an interview, but you feel certain the job will go to somebody else. Deep down you think: 'I know I won't get it. What's the point?' Your last-minute preparations will reflect your lack of motivation.

- How would you feel if you played for a local sports team, but were never picked? If you were certain other people would always be ahead of you – motivation would be lost, and you'd eventually quit the team.

- You really want to paint, but through school you were told: 'You're not creative. Don't bother with "arty" subjects and stick to something else.' Whenever you get the urge to paint, you dismiss it as pointless. Motivation is lost entirely.

Limiting beliefs lower expectations. We then struggle to value the potential rewards in life. As a result, procrastination becomes even more likely.

IN SUMMARY

Understanding the relationship between *effort*, *enjoyment*, *expectancy*, *delayed rewards* and *value* is key to boosting your motivation. Procrastination happens less when you:

- value the rewards your actions might bring

- transcend limiting beliefs, and improve your expectancy of success

- learn to value even delayed rewards

- decrease your perception of effort when taking action.

Everything takes *more effort* when the value of taking action is unclear. Let's explore this with another case study.

Case study: Henry's story

Henry, a former fitness instructor, was retraining to become an accountant. Already part-qualified, he found the work enjoyable and rewarding. Everything was going well... until recently: now his studies had ground to a halt.

Procrastination was a new experience for Henry. To gain more understanding, he was asked some simple questions. Here are his answers:

On a scale of 1–10, how much effort does it take to revise?

About a 6. It's hard work, but OK.

On a scale of 1–10, how much do you enjoy revising?

Honestly – about a 2. I'm not enjoying this module, and I find it really boring.

What rewards will the revision bring? On a scale of 1–10, how much do you value these rewards?

Massive rewards! When I'm qualified, I'll have a new career that's interesting and pays well – 10 out of 10!

Is there a delay between task and reward? If there is a delay, how does it affect your view of those rewards?

A delay of about three years! When I think about it, I don't really see passing this exam as rewarding at all.

On a scale of 1–10, how much do you expect to succeed?

Honestly, about a 4 out of 10. I'm worried that I keep reading it and rereading it but it's still not sinking in.

Reviewing Henry's answers, there are several problems:

▶ Studying is quite challenging; it requires significant *effort*.

▶ There is little *enjoyment*. This increases the effort it seems to take.

▶ Although Henry values his goal, there is a significant *delay* between action (studying for this exam) and reward (qualifying as an accountant). This clouds his understanding; he cannot see the *value* of studying. As a result, it takes even more effort.

▶ He is not convinced he will pass this exam. As a result, studying takes more effort still. It is hard to value a reward you do not *expect* to receive.

Viewed this way, Henry's procrastination is easy to understand. Consider your own difficulties for a moment. Are you discouraged by the *effort* everything seems to take? Do you genuinely believe your actions will be *rewarded*?

So far, we've explored the theory. Now, let's review the practical steps you can take. There are several techniques to choose from.

Valuing rewards

As we have learned, valuable rewards build motivation. Before starting any task, it is important to see this – otherwise you're likely to procrastinate. The following techniques are quick, simple and effective. Think clearly, avoid unnecessary cynicism, and your perceptions will change.

WHAT'S IN IT FOR ME?

Earlier, we read about Henry's recent difficulty with studying. Let's explore the approaches he could take to feel more motivated. We'll use the ABC model to describe the process:

▶ **Activating event:** sitting down to study.

▶ **Belief:** Henry thinks: 'I don't want to do this. It's really difficult – none of it makes sense!' He then pictures himself failing his exam.

▶ **Consequence:** a firm resistance to the idea of studying.

In this example, Henry talks himself out of studying. Contrast this with the following scenario:

▶ **Activating event:** sitting down to study.

▶ **Belief:** Henry thinks: 'Right, I'll get this out of the way and then I can relax for the rest of the night. It's really important that I pass this exam, and I know I'll get better if I spend time on it.' As he thinks this, Henry imagines passing his exam, and then settling down to study.

▶ **Consequence:** Henry feels determined to study.

Here, rather than focusing on the difficulties, Henry *values* the rewards. He then feels more motivated. If unclear on the rewards, ask yourself these questions:

▷ How does this action directly benefit me?

▷ What negative things will I avoid by acting?

So, Henry is primed to revise – but then hesitates. It is a tough module, and he could be having fun instead. At this point he asks:

▶ *How does this action directly benefit me?*

'Studying now means I'm getting better at this subject. I want to qualify as an accountant, and I need to pass this exam.'

'I'll feel good for making progress and taking action.'

▶ *What negative things will I avoid by acting?*

'I'll avoid failing the exam (or putting it off indefinitely!)'

'I'll avoid feeling bad about procrastinating.'

By affirming the rewards, he understands the value. As we have seen, this increases our motivation:

▶ *How does this action directly benefit me?* Notice the word 'benefit'. In marketing theory, people sell benefits because they motivate us to buy. This question works on the same principle.

▶ *What negative things will I avoid by acting?* Procrastination leads to anxiety and torment, which you avoid by acting now. Also, you stave off future complications or difficulties – which is rewarding in itself.

Let's explore another technique. You may have heard the phrase: 'You don't know what you have until you lose it.' This powerful idea can change our understanding.

CONTRASTING – UNDERSTANDING THE NEED FOR CHANGE

So, Henry feels more motivated to study – but still he wavers. This next exercise helped massively. It unfolds over five simple steps and is very straightforward:

1 *Step 1 – indulge*:

   To begin, Henry considers the reward: how good it will feel when finished and he is able to relax without guilt, having risen to the challenge. He then imagines passing his exam, if it were happening now.

2 *Step 2 – dwell*:

   Henry then thinks about abandoning the goal and losing those rewards. He imagines sitting on his settee, feeling guilty and miserable. He keenly feels a sense of *missing out*.

3 *Step 3 – contrast*:

   He then evaluates the difference between the two situations, gauging the satisfaction of each. He understands the reality – studying has real *value*, whereas procrastination only leads to negative consequences.

4 *Step 4 – take responsibility*:

   Henry asks himself: 'Whose responsibility is it? Is anything stopping me or am I stopping myself?' He is in no doubt – studying is his responsibility. His choice is informed by the facts. Henry cannot deny the value of taking action, and he appreciates the cost of procrastination.

5 *Step 5 – act*:

   Finally, he sits down and starts revising, easing past some slight resistance by using the quick relaxation exercise. Because the benefits are clear, studying takes considerably less effort.

This simple technique clarifies the value in taking action. A word of caution: daydreaming about the rewards in life is *addictive*, and we can forget to take action. Do not get carried away!

HOW TO MAKE A START

Knowing how to start is a key skill. One approach is to *glide* into action. This is effective because it avoids provoking more stress. Instead, you move without *resistance*. Let's try an experiment.

In a moment, retrieve a bucket, bowl or large jug – and fill it *almost* to the brim. Then, slowly and carefully, carry it around your house for about a minute. You will need to:

- go quite slowly
- be deliberate
- concentrate
- avoid getting overexcited.

This only takes a minute and you will learn an important lesson. As you carry the water around, remember to be calm, careful and relaxed.

How did you do? It might seem abstract, but you've practised a form of effortless doing. Rather than pushing yourself, you have no choice but to take things *steadily*. This approach overcomes the stress we feel when taking action. Ease yourself into it, and stay calm and relaxed. Your stress levels then stay manageable.

You can use this approach for most tasks, and it can be highly effective.

WHAT TO DO WHEN SLIPPING

Even when you plan meticulously, ease past stress, and glide into action – you may still procrastinate. Anticipate some difficulty; it's frustrating and bewildering, but also inevitable.

When you struggle with procrastination – either before or during a task – consider the following:

- Do you feel tired, anxious, frustrated or confused?
- Has the task grown more complicated than anticipated?
- The task has grown larger than anticipated?
- Have you lost sight of the rewards?

Each of these factors will decrease motivation. It is important to keep negative beliefs in check, or the benefits of taking action become unclear. At such times, we need to regain focus. To achieve this, ask yourself these questions:

- On a scale of 1–10, how much effort will it take to complete *this task*?

- On a scale of 1–10, how much will I enjoy *this task*?

- What rewards will *this task* bring? On a scale of 1–10, how much do I value those rewards?

- Is there a delay between *this task* and the reward? If there is a delay, how does it affect my view of the reward?

- On a scale of 1–10, to what degree do I expect to succeed?

Remember – if we cannot see the point of taking action, motivation decreases and we're prone to procrastination. When struggling to stay motivated, carry out the following:

1 Relax and focus, using the quick relaxation exercise in Chapter 5.

2 Express any negative beliefs, using the techniques from Chapter 6.

3 Use the 'Rational affirmations' and the 'Spinning negative feelings' exercises from Chapter 7.

4 Reconnect with the *benefit* of taking action.

5 Then, focus on just the next 15 minutes, and *glide* into making a start.

Even the smallest tasks can grow more complex than first imagined – life rarely runs smoothly. Set out with optimism, but anticipate complications. This way, you'll be prepared.

REWARDING YOURSELF

As you make progress, it is important to reward yourself along the way. So:

- After each 15 minutes, give yourself a pat on the back.

- After 30 minutes, relax for 15 minutes (later, we will slightly increase the ratio between rest and work).

▶ Whenever you complete a task, acknowledge your progress – this is vital. Notice how your circumstances have improved through taking action.

This system of appropriate praise and reward fosters greater motivation. Understand and accept the cause and effect at play, and link small victories to your actions. Over time, you will associate action with reward.

Focus points

❋ *Mental contrasting is a powerful approach* based around the idea that 'you don't know what you have until you lose it'.

❋ *Connect with the rewards in life, but avoid too much daydreaming*; we can lose ourselves in our imagination. Use it to boost motivation, not to detract from it.

❋ *When taking action, glide into it slowly and deliberately.* Concentrate on staying calm and relaxed; your stress levels will stay manageable.

❋ *After each 15 minutes, give yourself a pat on the back.* After 30 minutes, or whenever you complete a task, acknowledge your progress and take a break – this improves motivation.

Putting this together

Let's put this together into one simple process. At first, this will take some time to complete. However, do not skip the steps; soon, you'll naturally think this way.

EXERCISE: GETTING A MINI-ACTION PLAN TOGETHER

▶ This exercise takes a couple of minutes.

▶ The aim of the exercise it to plan your next action.

▶ Use this exercise whenever you need to take action.

1 As always, start by asking yourself: 'What do I need to do next?'

▷ Is there a job that needs doing now?

▷ If not, select a task from your goal 'action plan'.

▷ Choose a task (or tasks) that you can work on for the next 30 minutes.

2 If you can finish the task(s) within 30 minutes, write down *all* of the steps required. If it will take longer, write down your action for the next 30 minutes – no longer.

3 Estimate how long it will take to complete the plan, and note how you'll cope with procrastination urges. See the list above: 'What to do when slipping'.

4 Identify the moments where you risk procrastination.

5 Ask yourself these questions. Keep your answers brief:

 ▷ 'How does this action directly benefit me?'

 ▷ 'What negative things will I avoid by acting?'

Again – it only takes a moment to complete this mini-action plan. As you progress through it, tick each step – or tick the whole plan when finished.

Figure 8.1 is a blank mini-action plan for you to photocopy or otherwise reproduce.

MINI-ACTION PLAN

(A) The steps I will take: _____
_____
_____

(B) How long I will be active for: _____

(C) How I will cope with the urge to procrastinate: _____
_____
_____

(D) When I might get the urge to procrastinate: _____
_____
_____

Figure 8.1 Blank mini-action plan

Alternatively, use your notebook, the headers looking
something like this:

MINI-ACTION PLAN

STEPS:

TIME:

COPE BY:

DANGER:

REWARDS:

When you have drawn up your mini-action plan, carry out the
following process:

EXERCISE: SIMPLE MOTIVATION PROCESS

▶ This exercise takes just a few minutes each time.

▶ The aim of the exercise it to feel ready to act.

▶ Carry this out multiple times over the next few days.

▶ Use this exercise whenever you need to take action.

▶ Record your experience using these ABC records or your
notebook.

1 With your mini-action plan to hand, dismiss any
procrastination excuses, express any negative beliefs, and use
the 'Spinning negative feelings' technique. This should take
less than 2–3 minutes.

2 Then, spend 30–60 seconds on the *contrasting* process:

▷ *Indulge*: think about having the rewards you have
identified. Let your imagination run wild, and enjoy them
as if happening now.

▷ *Dwell*: then, accept the reality of your current situation – you
do not have these rewards, and procrastination will deny
them to you. Plus, you will experience further problems.

▷ *Contrast:* compare these scenarios in your mind, and choose one!

▷ *Take responsibility:* ask yourself: 'Whose responsibility is it? Is anything stopping me, or am I stopping myself?'

3 Next, use the affirmation technique from Chapter 7: 'By *doing this now*, I am becoming healthier/happier/more successful/stronger/more confident, etc.'

4 Finally, slowly and steadily *glide* into starting the task. Stay relaxed and avoid creating internal stress. Just ease yourself into the first 15 minutes of action.

5 Work for 15 minutes and congratulate yourself for doing well. Restate the *rational affirmation* (see above), and carry on for another 15 minutes without pause. Then, take a 15-minute break. Avoid the temptation to prolong it.

6 If you become stressed at any point, use the quick relaxation exercise or the 'Spinning negative feelings' technique to stay calm and focused. Consider whether the task has become complicated, or if you've lost sight of the rewards. Either way, ease past these moments by following your mini-action plan.

7 When you have completed the task, or worked for 30 minutes, acknowledge the benefits to taking action. Then, make notes about the experience – using a photocopied ABC record or your notebook.

8 When you have completed the ABC record, repeat the process from the beginning, with a new mini-action plan.

By *contrasting*, *gliding* and *rewarding*, your ability to motivate yourself will improve. Keep your stress levels low as you act. The more relaxed you feel, the longer you will be able to work for.

After carrying out this exercise, make notes on the experience. Complete this exercise ten times before moving on to the next chapter.

Figure 8.2 is a blank ABC record for you to photocopy or otherwise reproduce.

Date and time:	
Activating situation:	*What task did you procrastinate about?*
	Were you finding it difficult to start a task / persevere with a task / complete a task / or get going again in between tasks?
	Were there any noteworthy cues (location, emotional state, last action, other people)?
Belief:	*How did you excuse your decision to procrastinate. What did you say, picture or feel?*
	What negative emotions did you feel when you focused on the task?
	What negative thoughts did you have about the task?
Consequence:	*Were you able to carry out your plan?*
	Were you able to 'spin' the feelings? What affirmation did you use? Did you remember to acknowledge your efforts after 15 and 30 minutes?

Figure 8.2 Blank ABC record

In an A5 notebook, you would want this information to take up one page:

Date and time:
Task:
Cues:
Excuse:
Emotions:
Technique results:
Affirmation:
Acknowledge effort:

Practise this exercise ten times over the next few days. As before, fill out the ABC record – around two or three ABC records per day. Writing down your answers is important; observation and reflection contribute towards your learning. Be thorough now and it will pay off.

Moving on

The ratio between effort and reward governs our motivation. Harness this, and you will procrastinate less. Use the techniques in this chapter with a variety of tasks, and give yourself time to learn. Eventually, they will prove incredibly effective.

Focus points

✸ *When tasks seem enjoyable and rewarding, motivation is easy to come by.* When they seem to take a lot of effort, motivation decreases.

✸ *Effort is subjective* – our perception of it changes according to factors. Value the rewards you hope to achieve, and everything takes less effort.

✸ *Break tasks into small chunks*, and acknowledge your progress – your motivation will increase.

* *Motivation weakens when we do not expect to succeed.* Remember to use the affirmation technique from Chapter 7.
* *Try to stay as relaxed as possible while working.* The less stressed you feel, the more likely you are to make progress. Relaxed action is key.

Next step

Remember: you will still procrastinate at times. However, allow yourself time to learn these new skills, and things will continue to improve. In the next chapter, we will look at further techniques to bolster motivation.

Enhancing motivation

In this chapter you will learn:

- ▶ *How to mitigate feelings of effort by adopting a few simple strategies*
- ▶ *How to boost your determination to complete a task*
- ▶ *How procrastination can become a habit and even an addiction, and how to break such a habit or addiction*
- ▶ *How to bring all the above techniques together as you continue to challenge your procrastination and take control.*

How do you feel?

1 Do you want to feel more motivated?

2 Are you often on 'autopilot'?

3 Do you wonder why you cannot control procrastination?

4 Does everything seem difficult?

5 Do you find yourself easily distracted?

In the previous chapter we explored the relationship between effort and reward, and the effect it has on motivation. We then looked at ways to foster motivation by *valuing* rewards. More focus means less delay.

Next, we will explore your relationship with *effort*. Nothing is set in stone, and your ability to take action can improve. We will then examine *compulsive procrastination*, and consider strategies to alleviate it. By the end of this chapter, you will have several new tools at your disposal.

Mitigating effort

Many people enjoy watching films at the cinema, but do not go as often as they would like. It takes effort to travel there, to arrive on time and buy a ticket, and then find a seat. For some, this seems like too much hassle. Motivation is lost.

Others think differently. They focus on the enjoyment – watching the film and relaxing. They ignore the effort required, and *just get on with it*. You, too, can learn to focus on the enjoyment, rather than on the hassle.

To illustrate how, let's consider a real-life example:

Case study: Tony's story

Tony had recently taken up jogging. He enjoyed it, and it helped him stay in shape. Recently, he'd decided to train for a half-marathon, but as winter drew in he struggled to feel motivated.

Tony believed he could only run 'when in the mood'. After a stressful day, or if conditions were murky, he would procrastinate. Running was strenuous enough; when it's cold, wet and windy, it just seemed like too much effort.

Tony was shown several techniques to change this. As a result, he made good progress. Let's review the techniques he tried.

The following techniques increase motivation by changing your relationship with effort. Read through each one carefully – how do they apply to *your* life?

PUTTING THINGS INTO PERSPECTIVE

So, imagine Tony hesitating about his run. It's a miserable winter's evening, and there are a thousand things he'd rather be doing.

Running in blustery conditions is no fun. However, Tony was advised to put it into perspective. It's just 30 minutes, and there are more difficult things in life. It will soon be over – he can then relax and feel satisfied with his achievement.

When we baulk at a certain task, it is worth checking:

▶ 'Am I blowing this out of proportion?'

▶ 'How much time will this actually take?'

▶ 'Is this really so difficult?'

Instead of reasoning things through, we sometimes make snap judgements. Put things back into perspective and gain a clearer view of the *actual* effort required. For instance, consider the following:

▶ Breaking up with somebody

▶ Being made redundant

▶ Moving house

▶ Attending an important job interview

▶ Completing a degree

▶ Recovering from illness or injury

and so on...

Compared to these tasks, running is easy. You might think this comparison is invalid, but it restores perspective – and that is important. Many things we procrastinate about are not *that* difficult.

Consider the tasks you regularly delay. Do you overestimate the effort required? When we respond emotionally, rather than think rationally, we make mountains out of molehills. Motivation increases with clearer perspective – it is an important skill to master.

FOCUS ON THE FIRST 15 MINUTES

You have been encouraged to organize *action* into 15- or 30-minute blocks. There is good reason for this. When *sizing up* a task, we risk becoming discouraged – particularly if we overburden ourselves. Our heart sinks as we think, 'It's too much!' Motivation is lost and we start to procrastinate.

Instead, just focus on the first few steps and get started. For Tony, this meant thinking: 'Right! Shoes on. Out of the door. Get the first 15 minutes over with, and it's all downhill from there.' Tony discouraged himself when he thought about the whole run. By concentrating on the first few steps, getting out of the door was much easier.

When weighing up action, it helps to think:

▶ 'Let's just concentrate on the first 15 minutes.'

▶ 'Once I get going this will be easy.'

▶ 'I'll be fine when I'm up and running!'

Focus on manageable chunks rather than the unmanageable whole. Your motivation will improve because your assessment of the effort concerned will encompass only the start.

A SPOONFUL OF SUGAR

Some tasks are just impossible to love. Imagine applying for a job: although an excellent opportunity, there are too many forms to complete. And you're not certain to get an interview. Plus you're quite happy in your current role, and suddenly it seems a bit... well, pointless. You put it off until the last minute, and perhaps indefinitely. It is an opportunity missed.

Sometimes, comforting yourself *during* the task helps. You could think: 'OK – I'll treat myself to an extra-large coffee as I fill this out.' This would help, as would listening to your favourite music and sitting in a comfy chair. Sweetening the bitter pill works.

There *is* a risk to this approach. You could enjoy the coffee and listen to music without completing the application! You need to remind yourself: 'Yes – but I'll enjoy these things *so much more* if I get this task out of the way as well.' Comfort without reward feels hollow.

WHISTLE WHILE YOU WORK

If you don't enjoy something, why do it? This *is* a fair question, but if you only did things you enjoy, your life would quickly fall into disrepair. We have to do things we'd prefer to avoid. But that need not mean a life of misery. It pays to find the positive in our experiences.

For Tony, this meant thinking: 'Right! I'm going to really push myself tonight.' Driving forward and beating the elements enlivened his running experience. It was more enjoyable, and felt less of a chore. It's a question of where you place your *focus*.

Focus on the enjoyable rather than the difficult or unpleasant, and *time* flies by. Either struggle to run through the biting cold, legs miserable with pain. Or feel *alive*; the wind at your back, racing from one lamp post to the next. You can choose.

Everything becomes much easier when you accentuate the positive:

▶ 'How can I make this fun?'

▶ 'What can I focus on to enjoy?'

▶ 'How can I turn this into a game?'

▶ 'What similar things do I enjoy, and can I feel the same about this?'

Some activities are more enjoyable than others (of course). However – consider these approaches:

▶ *Make a game out of it.* By using your imagination, you can turn *most* tasks into a type of game. We routinely do this as children; tap into that ability and time flies by – particularly repetitive or boring tasks.

▶ *Selective focusing.* We are naturally *tunnel-visioned*. Turn this to your advantage and focus on the pleasurable. Pay less attention to the negative elements, and tasks become much easier.

▶ *Make it feel like a task you enjoy.* Identify the commonality between unpleasant and enjoyable tasks. For example, if you enjoy ironing but hate de-cluttering – concentrate on the abstract similarities. Ironing involves sorting, processing and completing, so view de-cluttering in the same way. You will feel different, and taking action becomes easier.

Tasks are made more enjoyable by focusing on the positive (admittedly this is not possible with all tasks – completing a tax return, for example). We can be overly cynical about things, which only corrodes our motivation. When trying to overcome procrastination, cynicism is an expensive luxury you cannot afford.

CREATE COMPETITION

Some people excel *when competing* – either against others or themselves. In Tony's case, this meant striving to beat previous times despite the difficult conditions. He also thought about beating other runners, and how good that would feel. In the right circumstances, competition dramatically changes our relationship with effort. Thoughts worth considering:

▶ 'How can I turn this into a competition?'

▶ 'I am going to do better than ever tonight!'

▶ 'C'mon! I'll prove I can do this!'

Competition, in the right circumstances, makes us strive harder. We are less concerned about effort. For some people, competition makes a huge difference.

Quick fix: Boost your energy

Our perceptions are affected by our energy levels. Feeling tired, stressed or hung-over exacerbates procrastination. Improving your energy always helps. If you frequently feel tired or lethargic – consider the following:

* Drink two quick glasses of water.
* Splash cold water on your face.
* Listen to loud music and dance around for five minutes.
* Eat a banana!
* Spend a bit of time de-cluttering something.

If your low energy runs deeper than this, consider a health check-up, nutritional advice, your sleeping patterns, and your relationship with exercise. You will benefit by focusing on your lifestyle. The techniques in this book can book can help.

IN SUMMARY

Your *perception* of effort determines your response to it. Whenever you sigh and feel reluctant, procrastination becomes more likely. We all have a 'sulky teenager' mode, and it does not help us achieve great things in life.

Change your emotional responses, and action becomes easier. Otherwise, you will remain stuck – which, eventually, you will come to regret. Now is the right time to change the way you think.

Read through the list once more and keep an open mind. How can *you* do things differently? Focus on the possibilities. Later, we will put these techniques into action. For now, let's look at another method of *getting started*.

Focus points

* *It is easy for us to make mountains out of molehills.* Keep things in perspective, and you will be less discouraged.
* *Focus on manageable chunks, and your motivation will improve.* Nothing daunts us more than thinking about the size of the task ahead.

* *When struggling with unpleasant tasks, it helps to 'sweeten the bitter pill'.* Think of ways you can increase your comfort when tackling things you'd prefer to avoid.
* *Make use of your imagination, and turn tasks into a game.* This works particularly well with repetitive or boring tasks.
* *Our focus tends to be quite narrow.* Rather than focusing on the difficulties, accentuate the positive and ignore the negative.
* *We tend to strive harder when in competition – either with ourselves or others.* We are then less concerned with the effort required.

Boosting your determination

In the previous chapter you learned how to *glide* into action. This technique helps you to ease past stress – a significant cause of procrastination. By tiptoeing past your anxiety and frustration, you are free to just get on with it.

Let's discuss an alternative approach to getting started. In this next exercise, you will boost your feelings of determination. This method is helpful when feeling discouraged by challenging tasks.

In Chapter 7 you learned how to 'spin' feelings. By spinning negative feelings backwards, you reduced their intensity. This next technique is similar. You will learn how to increase your determination.

EXERCISE: SPINNING MOTIVATED FEELINGS

▶ This exercise takes five minutes to learn, and a minute or so to do; practise it often.

▶ The aim is to observe your feelings in a certain way and learn to change them.

▶ When you get the hang of this exercise, you'll realize it is really simple.

▶ Read through the steps first and familiarize yourself with them.

▶ Use this exercise whenever you need to boost your motivation.

1 Select a task you want to complete. Draw up a mini-action plan and focus on that task now.

2 Think about the rewards this task will bring, and how much you'd enjoy them; how your circumstances will improve as a result, and how you'll be able to relax afterwards.

3 Imagine this in vivid detail until you feel motivated and determined to make a start. Then, ask yourself: 'What's happening in my body?' Answer the following questions:

   ▷ Where is the location of the feeling in my body (stomach, chest, face, cheeks, shoulders, etc.)?

   ▷ How does the feeling move? Is it a rising feeling or a sinking feeling? Is it a tight knot, spinning clockwise or anticlockwise?

   ▷ Does the feeling move quickly or slowly?

   ▷ What texture does the feeling have? Smooth, fuzzy, rough, tingly, spiky, or texture-*less*?

   ▷ Is the feeling narrow or wide? Is it hotter or colder than the rest of your body?

   ▷ How intense is the feeling on a scale of 1–10? How much pressure does it generate, or is the feeling light?

   ▷ If the feeling had a colour, what colour would it be? (Just guess!)

To answer these questions fully, you may need to carry out these steps several times.

4 Repeat steps 1–3 and feel *determined*. Then, imagine you can reach into the feeling and push it, so it moves strongly through your body *in the same direction*. Each time you inhale, attempt the following:

   ▷ Imagine growing more determined and motivated.

   ▷ Imagine the feelings moving more quickly, and with greater depth and power.

   ▷ Imagine the feelings growing wider and more intense.

   ▷ If the feeling is moving from your stomach to your chest (for example), push it up and beyond, into your shoulders and your face.

▷ What colour did you give the feeling? Make that colour more vibrant and intense.

5   Spend a couple of minutes spinning the positive feeling around your body. Your concentration will naturally wax and wane. If you lose focus, concentrate on the rewards and reconnect with the feelings.

6   Finally, think about making a start and being really determined. Imagine this clearly in your mind, and tell yourself: 'By starting this now, I am getting what I want in life.'

Get to grips with this technique, and you can boost your determination when required. Use it often: weaken procrastination urges by spinning them backwards, and boost motivated feelings by pushing them forwards. This excellent tool makes a huge difference to procrastination.

With practice you could easily find yourself starting tasks *at will*. However, there is still one factor standing in our way – and perhaps it is the most dangerous of all.

Habits and addiction

Despite the exercises in this book, there is a good chance that you still procrastinate frequently. To understand this we must consider your relationship with delay. So to begin – ask yourself: When was the last time you had to concentrate while tying your shoelaces?

UNDERSTANDING HABITS

Tying your shoelaces involves seven steps, performed in a particular order. You can tie them with your eyes closed, and while thinking about something else entirely. You do not need to concentrate on the task, and this is a good thing. If we had to concentrate on every simple thing we did, life would be tiring – and dangerous.

The human brain strives to automate routine procedures. Repetitive actions are 'chunked' together so they flow automatically. To your brain, the seven steps of tying your shoelaces is a single *routine*. It unfolds seamlessly, and you're free to think about other things. Habits are an incredibly efficient way of getting things done.

As this efficiency is so important, our brains attempt to turn all repetitive action into habits. There is no differentiation between the habits which help, and those habits which hold us back. Our brain just automates as much as possible. Sometimes, this causes real problems.

HOW DO HABITS WORK?

All habits unfold via a three-step process: there is a *cue*, a *routine* and a *reward*.

For example, you were once taught to check for traffic before crossing a road. This now happens without too much conscious effort. This useful habit is almost automatic, but there *is* a decision for the brain to make. When you arrive by the roadside, your brain looks for a *cue* – a factor, or combination of factors, which helps your brain decide on which *routine* to use next.

▶ A busy road will *cue* your brain to deploy the 'waiting by the road' routine. After a while, the road is rechecked, and again your brain decides what to do next.

▶ A clear road cues the brain to deploy the 'crossing the road' routine. When finished, your brain then checks to make sure everything is as expected. This is known as the *reward*. In our example of crossing the road, you are rewarded by arriving at the other side.

The three-step process of *cue*, *routine* and *reward* has functioned perfectly. This activity unfolds within moments, and with little conscious effort or awareness on your part. Here is a quick summary:

The waiting by the road habit:

▶ **Cue:** the road is busy.

▶ **Routine:** wait until it is clear.

▶ **Reward:** avoid being hurt by traffic.

The crossing the road habit:

▶ **Cue:** the road is clear.

▶ **Routine:** cross the road quickly.

▶ **Reward:** arrive on the other side.

We rely on hundreds of these habits to get by. Without them, our consciousness would be overwhelmed. Instead, habits are deployed with *little* awareness. In the case of procrastination, as you can imagine, this lack of awareness is especially problematic.

With repetition, habits become more and more entrenched. People who procrastinate frequently acquire *an habitual procrastination routine*. And it unfolds without the need for a conscious decision.

Read through the following examples. Do you identify with these scenarios?

The 'Facebook' habit:

▶ **Cue:** sitting at your computer – you have studying to do.

▶ **Routine:** using your computer *cues* the brain to log into Facebook – other tasks are put to one side.

▶ **Reward:** Facebook is open – all is as it should be.

As discussed, procrastination *is* rewarding from one perspective – it grants us a temporary respite from stress. From a habit-forming perspective, our brain expects certain results when habitual routines are deployed. It then thinks: 'Great, everything is as it should be...'

The 'putting things off until tomorrow' habit:

Cue: feeling bad about a task you do not wish to do.

Routine: the reluctant feelings *cue* the brain to devise an excuse: 'I'll do it later.' This unfolds with lightning speed, and we turn our attention to other things.

Reward: avoid the cause of the stress – all is as it should be.

Here, our habit-forming brain has automated stress avoidance, and excuses are automatic. Let's look at a final example.

The 'refusing action' habit:

▶ **Cue:** spotting a task that needs doing, e.g. loading the dishwasher.

▶ **Routine:** knowing you have a task to complete *cues* the brain to reject the idea. You 'find yourself' doing something else instead.

▶ **Reward:** avoid the stress of sorting something out – all is as it should be.

The pattern is easy to spot. Repeatedly avoid taking action, and your brain will automate the process. This unfolds *unconsciously*, and you find yourself acting against your best interests.

Habits are especially powerful when driven by emotional need; they can completely override our logic. Because procrastination alleviates stress – albeit temporarily – we *are* emotionally invested in the outcome. According to some research, emotionally charged habits are indistinguishable from *addiction*.

Procrastination can be addictive

Ask any recovering addict, and they will say there no such thing as 'just once'. Inevitably, *just once* is the thin end of the wedge. Breaking their abstinence means their addiction will take over. Before long, it will be at its uncontrollable worst.

For example – some people can smoke occasionally, but most 'smokers' quickly become addicted. Their addiction takes over their life, driving much of their thought, their feelings and their behaviour.

In such cases, stopping smoking means *complete abstinence*. Trying to cut down doesn't really work. In response to certain cues – for example, stress or boredom – their urge to smoke will creep back and eventually take over. To stop smoking, they have to cut out the cigarettes completely.

The same principle applies to recovering alcoholics, gambling addicts, drug addicts, people who self-harm, and workaholics. 'Just once' is an illusion; the old routines *will* take over. The only way people overcome their addiction is by accepting this reality. Emotionally charged habits are impossible to control.

So – for a moment, consider your relationship with procrastination. Think about the wasted hours, the irrational decisions; the stress, anxiety and missed opportunities. Think about the broken promises and ask yourself: Can you control this entrenched, emotionally charged habit? What does the evidence suggest?

This is the most damaging aspect of procrastination. Just a moment's delay can turn in to hours of damaging and debilitating procrastination. The risk associated with 'just five minutes' is impossible to overstate. Most likely, it *will* lead to significant delay. Again – review the evidence. What does it suggest?

To really turn your procrastination around, accept your inability to control it when it takes hold. This way, your mind is alert to the dangers you face. There is no such thing as:

► 'I'll just check my emails first.'

► 'I'll just quickly log onto Facebook.'

► 'I'll just have a quick read through the paper.'

► 'I'll just make a cup of tea.'

► 'I'm hungry, I'll just have a snack first.'

► 'I just have to make some phone calls first.'

► 'I just need to run to the shops.'

And so on… These excuses enable your brain to deploy automatic procrastination routines regardless of your best interests. Your brain believes it is being efficient and meeting your needs. In fact it is ruining your life.

When you feel the urge to procrastinate, recognize it for what it is. Abstain from needless delay, and your procrastination will diminish significantly.

A DISTRACTED LIFE

We have access to more distractions than ever: TV, the Internet, computer games, Kindles, text messaging, YouTube, iPods, iPads, Twitter, Facebook... It is a wonder that anything gets done at all!

When you have *things to do*, eliminate as many temptations as possible. If you're keen to spend the next few hours gardening or finishing an essay, to prepare you could do the following:

▶ Unplug your TV from the power socket, the aerial, your games console and/or DVD player.

▶ Place your phone, your iPad and your half-read novel in a cupboard somewhere.

▶ Use a website like www.rescuetime.com to block access to Twitter and Facebook.

And so on...

You might think: 'Well, that's all a bit extreme, isn't it?' But again – an alcoholic removes temptation because they know one drink will lead to many. Procrastination *is* addictive. One slip could lead to countless lost hours.

For many, accepting the reality of their addiction is enough. Alert to the importance of avoiding unnecessary delays, they just do not allow themselves to start. Others need to be more careful.

Remove distractions and this becomes easier. If you reject this idea as nonsense or unnecessary, consider the true reasons for your conclusion. Believing you can control procrastination, when the evidence suggests otherwise, hints at an unwillingness to accept the truth.

Quick fix: Remove distractions

Cut down on interruptions as much as possible. For instance, rather than checking your email every 10–20 minutes, check it just three times per day: in the morning, after lunch and in the evening.

Are you always glued to your mobile? Hide it away somewhere and again check it just two or three times per day. So much time is wasted by replying to messages as they're received. Mostly, this is just procrastination.

Get into the habit of replying to emails, voicemails and texts at certain times. You will be amazed at how much time you free up. Despite what you may think, the world will survive in your absence.

So, consider removing all distractions when you need to get things done. In the meantime, here is an excellent technique for combating habitual procrastination. It is very, very simple.

EXERCISE: PAUSE FOR TEN SECONDS

▶ This exercise takes just moments.

▶ The aim is to break the habitual cycle of cue – routine – reward.

▶ Read through the steps first and familiarize yourself with them.

▶ Use it whenever you get the urge to delay.

1 Whenever you need to get something done, ensure all distractions are inconvenient to access. Putting that extra obstacle in your way gives you more time to think.

▷ Unplug the TV (and games console, DVD, etc.) from the power socket.

▷ Log out of all distracting websites: Facebook, email, Twitter, etc.

▷ Computer games a problem? Create a new folder on your desktop, and hide shortcuts to distracting software.

▷ Tempted by a favourite book? Put it in a cupboard in a different room.

▷ Hide away your smartphone.

And so on. Make it difficult to access to typical distractions.

2 *Whenever* you get the urge to delay or avoid something, acknowledge the urge as an irrational habit. There was a *cue*, and now your brain is trying to deploy a *routine*. There is no such thing as 'I'll just do this for five minutes.' One small delay could derail your whole day.

3 Next, do nothing other than to slowly count down from 10 to 1. Each time you exhale, relax your shoulders and torso,

and focus. Tell yourself: 'I cannot control procrastination. It is better to do something else.'

4 Finally, focus on taking action for just 15 minutes. Once you're started, it quickly becomes easier. Remember: time *is* your most precious resource.

This simple technique breaks the procrastination habit. With repetition, habitual procrastination will become much weaker.

Focus points

- *Life would be impossible if we had to concentrate on everything.* As a result, our brain automates repetitive behaviours, turning them in to habits.
- *All habits unfold via a three-step process: a cue, a routine and a reward.* Automated habits are deployed with little conscious awareness.
- *With repetition, habits become more and more entrenched.* Your brain has a 'procrastination habit', which is deployed without your conscious input.
- *Ask yourself: 'Can I control my procrastination?'* What does the evidence suggest? Are you in control, or does it control you?
- *Be wary of delay.* It will take over your life whenever it can.
- *Appreciate the importance of rejecting procrastination – before you start.* As a result, you will avoid grinding to a halt.

Putting this together

Life is not supposed to be a relentless struggle. By using the techniques in this book, you could teach yourself to complete task after task, striving for reward after reward. You could be the happiest and most fulfilled human on the planet. Everything would be perfect!

Except – nothing could be further from the truth. You are not a robot, and the grinding pursuit of relentless happiness will only leave you miserable. The key, as always, is balance. In the next chapter, we will explore these themes in more detail. For now, pay consideration to these factors:

- It is important to rest and play – at least for a couple of hours each day.
- It is important to do new things from time to time. Avoid over-regulating your life.

Again, it is a question of balance.

We have covered a lot of ground in the past two chapters, so let's put these recommendations into action. As previously, start with a mini-action plan.

EXERCISE: GETTING A MINI-ACTION PLAN TOGETHER

▶ This exercise takes just a minute.

▶ The aim of the exercise it to plan your next action.

▶ Use this exercise whenever you need to take action.

1 As always, start by asking yourself: 'What do I need to do next?'

  ▷ Is there a job that needs doing now?

  ▷ If not, select a task from your goal 'action plan'.

  ▷ Choose a task (or tasks) that you can work on for the next 45 minutes.

2 Write down the steps you will take for the next 45 minutes – no longer. Use action-oriented words, and be specific.

3 Estimate how long it will take to complete the plan (maximum: 45 minutes), and note how you'll cope with procrastination urges.

4 Identify the moments where you risk procrastination.

5 Ask yourself these questions. Keep your answers brief:

  ▷ 'How does this action directly benefit me?'

  ▷ 'What negative consequences will I avoid by acting?'

6 Finally, ask yourself: 'How can I make this seem like less effort?' Again keeping your answers brief. Here are some ideas:

  ▷ 'Do I need to put this into perspective?'

  ▷ 'Can I focus on the first 15 minutes?'

  ▷ 'Do I need to add a "spoonful of sugar"?'

  ▷ 'Can I turn it into a game?'

  ▷ 'What positive elements can I focus on?'

▷ 'Can I make this seem like a task I *do* enjoy?'

▷ 'Can I create competition?'

Completing this mini-action plan takes moments, but it will keep you on track. Remember, break steps down into smaller chunks when required. As you progress through your plan, tick each step when completed – or tick the whole plan when finished.

Figure 9.1 is a blank plan for you to photocopy or otherwise reproduce.

MINI-ACTION PLAN

(A) The steps I will take: _____

_____

_____

(B) How long I will be active for: _____

_____

_____

(C) How I will cope with the urge to procrastinate: _____

_____

_____

(D) When I might get the urge to procrastinate: _____

_____

_____

(E) How this task will reward me: _____

_____

_____

(F) How I can make this seem like less effort: _____

_____

_____

Figure 9.1 Blank mini-action plan

Alternatively, use your notebook, the headers looking something like this:

MINI-ACTION PLAN

STEPS:

TIME:

COPE BY:

DANGER:

REWARDS:

LESS EFFORT:

When you have your mini-action plan to hand, move on to the following exercise.

EXERCISE: ENHANCED MOTIVATION PROCESS

▶ This exercise takes just a few minutes each time.

▶ The aim of the exercise is to feel motivated and ready to start taking action.

▶ Use this exercise whenever you are procrastinating or have a task to do.

▶ Carry this out multiple times over the next few days. Record your experience using the ABC records from this chapter or your notebook.

1 As before, with your mini-action plan to hand, dismiss any procrastination excuses, express any negative beliefs, and use the 'Spinning negative feelings' technique. In total, Step 1 should take 2–3 minutes.

2 Then, spend 30–60 seconds on the 'Contrasting' exercise:

▷ *Indulge*: think about having the rewards you've identified. Let your imagination run wild, and daydream about the benefits.

▷ *Dwell:* then, accept the reality of your current situation – you do not have these rewards, and procrastination will deny you of them (while bringing other complications).

▷ *Contrast:* compare these scenarios in your mind, and choose one!

▷ *Take responsibility:* ask yourself: 'Whose responsibility is it? Is anything stopping me, or am I stopping myself?'

3 Then, use the affirmation technique from Chapter 7: 'By *doing this now*, I am becoming healthier/happier/more successful/stronger/more confident, etc.'

4 Next, make sure you're keeping the task in perspective. Ask yourself:

▷ 'Am I blowing this out of proportion?'

▷ 'How much time will this actually take?'

▷ 'Is this really so difficult?'

It is important to focus on the steps you've written down and *not* the task as a whole – particularly if it is a large or complicated job. Put the future out of your mind, and focus on the next 15 minutes only.

5 Remember – any urge to delay could be an emotionally charged habit. Pause for ten seconds before delaying *anything*, and remember to view even the slightest delay as dangerous. Once started, you will not find it easy to stop.

6 When you drew up your mini-action plan, you decided how to make the task more enjoyable. Which approach did you choose?

▷ **A spoonful of sugar:** is there some way of making the experience more enjoyable?

▷ **Turn it into a game:** by using your imagination you can turn most tasks into a game. 'Washing-up Olympics', anyone?

▷ **Focus on the positive aspects:** many tasks involve some positive element – consider it a chore, or focus on the positive.

▷ **Make it feel like a different job you enjoy:** some tasks we hate are often similar to tasks we enjoy. Can you change the way you look at it?

▷ **Create competition:** for many people, creating a sense of competition – with ourselves or other people – boosts motivation.

▷ **Boost your energy:** have a slug of water or jump around for a bit to get your energy going – it will help.

7 Then, use the 'Spinning motivated feelings' exercise to fire yourself up and get started.

8 Aim to work for 15 minutes or so. Congratulate yourself for doing well, and carry on for a second 15 minutes. Congratulate yourself once more and complete a further 15 minutes. Then take a well-earned 15-minute rest.

Remember – when you take a break, keep it to 15 minutes *only* – it is all too easy for it to spiral out of control, costing you hours.

9 If you become stressed at any point, use the quick relaxation exercise or the 'Spinning negative feelings' exercise. Stay calm and focused. The urge to stop could mean the task has become complicated, or you've lost sight of the rewards. Perhaps you don't know what to do next, or it feels like too much effort?

10 Either way, ease past these moments by following your mini-action plan. Remember: procrastination is addictive. If you feel the urge to procrastinate at any point, pause for ten seconds before doing anything.

After completing 45 minutes, acknowledge your success and remember to congratulate yourself. Then, make notes about the experience using a photocopied ABC record or your notebook. Then, repeat the process from the beginning, with a new mini-action plan.

This expanded exercise now includes techniques to mitigate effort. It will seem a bit longwinded at first, but practise each step thoroughly – it only takes 2–3 minutes. In time, these steps will become habitual and you'll complete them within moments. Mastery takes repetition, so avoid skipping ahead.

Follow these steps as much as possible over the next few days. Each time you complete a task – or 45 minutes of positive action – write down your results. This will be the last set of ABC sheets you need to complete.

Expect to struggle on occasion, particularly at first. Do not be discouraged. Give yourself the time and space you need to learn these new skills. Complete this process at least ten times before moving on to the next chapter.

In an A5 notebook, you would want this information to take up one page:

Date and time:

Task:

Cues:

Excuse:

Emotions:

Technique results:

Affirmation:

Acknowledge effort:

As before, filling out this sheet will take 2–3 minutes. It is still important to make notes about your experiences; you will learn by doing so.

Moving on

Master the exercises in this chapter, and you could motivate yourself to do almost anything. However – remember that procrastination is addictive. Avoid spiralling delay by *pausing for 10 seconds* when necessary. With practice, you could be well on the road to recovery.

Figure 9.2 is the blank ABC record for you to photocopy or otherwise reproduce.

Date and time:	
Activating situation:	*What task did you procrastinate about?* *Were you finding it difficult to start a task / persevere with a task / complete a task / or get going again in between tasks?* *Were there any noteworthy cues (location, emotional state, last action, other people)?*
Belief:	*How did you excuse your decision to procrastinate. What did you say, picture or feel?* *What negative emotions did you feel when you focused on the task?* *What negative thoughts did you have about the task?*
Consequence:	*Were you able to carry out your plan?* *Were you able to 'spin' the feelings? What affirmation did you use? Did you remember to acknowledge your efforts after 15, 30 and 45 minutes?*

Figure 9.2 Blank ABC record

Focus points

* *We often overestimate the effort tasks will take.* Putting things into perspective stops us from feeling discouraged. Focus on just the first few steps, and avoid becoming overwhelmed.
* *Action can be made more enjoyable.* Perhaps you need a 'spoonful of sugar', or maybe you can turn it into a game. Can you accentuate the positive, and pay less attention to the negative? Master these skills, and your motivation will increase.
* *For many, creating competition – with others or with ourselves – boosts motivation.* Challenge yourself to do something, and you may procrastinate less.
* *In previous chapters you learned to spin feelings in your body.* Spin positive, motivated feelings and they become stronger, which helps us to make a start.
* *Our brains automate repetitive action.* Can you really control procrastination? Acknowledge the danger in starting, and it becomes much easier to avoid. Remind yourself: 'I cannot control procrastination. It is better to do something else.'

Next step

Although you have practised many skills to alleviate chronic procrastination, you are still at the beginning of this journey. To master what you have learned so far, more practice is necessary.

In the next chapter, we will revisit goal-setting, and discuss how you can use these new skills to improve your life. The impact could be immeasurable. For now, practise what you have learned so far.

A motivated future

In this chapter you will learn:

- ▶ *How to find 'prime time' for you to use to work towards your goals*
- ▶ *How to track your goals as you work towards them*
- ▶ *The importance of 'bouncing back' after a period of negativity and renewed procrastination*
- ▶ *The importance of having passion*
- ▶ *How to identify your key values*
- ▶ *How to 'clear the decks' so that you concentrate on your goals*
- ▶ *How to say 'no'*
- ▶ *How to set big, life-changing goals.*

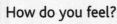

How do you feel?

1 Do you wonder where to start?

2 Do you wish you could say 'no'?

3 Are life's problems holding you back?

4 Wouldn't you want to do something important with your life?

5 Do you want to feel more confident?

Achieving a happy and balanced life is no easy task. Whether our dreams are grandiose or straightforward, at some point we have to push ourselves. This means rising to the challenge and pressing on. For some of us, this is hard to accept.

We yearn for the easier option, the short-cut and the quick fix; but there is another way. As Bruce Lee once wrote: 'Do not pray for an easy life. Pray for the strength to endure a difficult one.' With a little practice, you can acquire all the strength you need.

In this chapter, we will explore the possibilities for your future – a life lived true to your values.

Goals revisited

In Chapter 2 we discussed well-formed goals. You learned how to define *specific steps* and *measurable outcomes*, and to ensure your goals are attainable, relevant and time-based. Thoroughly defined goals give direction in life. Without them, we can only be aimless.

Did you define a practice goal in Chapter 2? Some will have ignored this advice, although it is not too late to start. If you truly want to overcome procrastination, you must write down your goals. Then, you can identify the best time to act.

Scheduling

Finding the time to work towards our goals is difficult. There are several approaches to this, ranging from the simple to the complex. Here, we'll keep it simple. Later, you can always look into more sophisticated techniques.

EXERCISE: SIMPLE SCHEDULING

▶ This exercise takes about ten minutes.

▶ The aim is to identify your 'prime time' for getting things done.

▶ Use this exercise whenever you need to identify your spare time.

1 To begin, take a blank A4 sheet of paper (or set up a Word document) and create seven columns, headed 'Monday' through to 'Sunday'.

2 Then, briefly sketch out your typical working week. The time you're up; the time you set off for work; the time you take a lunch-break; the time you arrive home; the time it takes to change, shower, eat and so on. Complete this process for Monday–Friday.

   If you work shifts or unusual hours, follow the same process for each shift pattern. The aim is the same: to create an overview of your typical working week.

3 Then, complete the same process for Saturday and Sunday. Write down your typical rising time, and list the commitments, tasks and errands that usually take place each weekend.

   Only spend 5–10 minutes on this. You can tighten it up as you go along.

4 Next, identify the spare time available each day. Focus on 'chunks of time', e.g. 7–8 a.m., Monday to Friday; 8–10 p.m., Monday to Thursday; 12 noon – 8 p.m., Saturday and Sunday. This is your 'prime time' for action.

5 Finally, type up the list of available timeslots on a single sheet of A4 paper, and pin the list next to your goals and action plan. For example:

   ▷ Monday: 7–8 a.m.; 12 noon – 1 p.m.; 8–10 p.m.

   ▷ Tuesday: 7–8 a.m.; 12 noon – 1 p.m.

   ▷ Wednesday: 7–8 a.m.; 12 noon – 1 p.m.; 8–10 p.m.

And so on...

6   You now know your available free time each week. When
    you arrive at these times, read through your action plan
    and work on the most important tasks. If you're uncertain,
    choose the *largest* task. Build motivation using the techniques
    in this book. Your 'prime time' is precious – value it.

Most people have spare time before work, perhaps at lunch,
and in the evening. There should also be some time on
Saturday, chores not withstanding; and some time on Sunday.
In Chapter 2 you completed the exercise: 'How much time
do I really have?' You may have felt shocked to see how little
time you have for yourself. Viewing your commitments in this
way can also be dispiriting. This is another reason to reject
unnecessary delay.

This exercise identifies chunks of available time. You can use it
to identify your prime time during work, around your studies,
and so on. It always helps to have a firm grip on the time
available to you.

To recap:

▶ Work out what you do each week.

▶ Identify the gaps around your regular activity (your 'prime
  time').

▶ Write those gaps down and display them somewhere visible.

▶ When those times arrive, choose the most important task
  from your action plan (if in doubt, choose the *biggest* task).

Use the techniques in this book to get started.

There *are* more complex scheduling systems available. Once you
get the hang of this, you can always try something a bit more
sophisticated.

Despite identifying the best time to act, and knowing what to do
next, you will still procrastinate – albeit less frequently. Tiredness,
confusion, discouragement and old habits will sometimes derail
you. However, master the techniques in this book and chronic
procrastination should become a thing of the past.

To ensure this, you need to track your progress. Then you can adjust your efforts as required.

Goal-tracking

It is vital to track your goals. To do this, you need a visible record of your progress. Download a free 'printable monthly calendar' – one month per sheet – from the Internet. Pin this next to your goal worksheet and action plan.

Then, using a notepad or a smartphone, keep track of each 45-minute spell you complete. Record the final tally on your calendar each day. Only record the time you spend working towards your goal, not other things.

For some goals, it helps to track the successes you have each day. For instance, if you aim to stick to a diet – mark each successful day with a tick. Be honest with yourself, and do not abandon this approach because you don't like the results. Accept the reality of your action or *in*action, and adjust your efforts accordingly. A *visible* calendar is important for this reason.

SET A TARGET

How much time could you reasonably spend on your goals each day? Can you work in the week, at weekends, or both? Set yourself targets, and aim to hit them. Miss the target repeatedly, and there is obviously a problem. Ask yourself: 'Where am I going wrong?'

When you slip, it is important to *keep going*. Resilience is the key ingredient to achieving any goal.

Bouncing back

Despite your best efforts, you will still procrastinate occasionally. Even the best of us struggle from time to time. No matter how strong you become, constant perfection is unattainable.

Expect difficulty and failure – it is inevitable, especially when trying to achieve important goals. This is not overly pessimistic. True pessimism would mean feeling unable to cope. When life knocks you down you have two choices: stop completely – or keep going.

It is not unhealthy to express negative feelings for a spell. However, prolong your upset and vitality drains away. A week or two of helplessness can quickly become weeks or months. Misery can be as addictive as delay.

In the previous chapter, you learned how to focus on what you want and spin motivated feelings through your body. Whenever you struggle or fail, let yourself recover and then concentrate on feeling more determined.

Typical setbacks:

- You realize you've been procrastinating for several hours.
- You've just binged on sugary treats.
- You've received yet another rejection letter through the post.
- You've just failed an essay you worked really hard on.
- A friend who you trust just won't return your phone calls for some reason.
- You've spent all week decorating your house. Now you realize you hate every bit of it.
- You are in trouble at work for something you haven't done.

At such times, switch your focus away from pain and disappointment and become determined to explore the opportunities you *do* have in life. It will take practice, and remember: allow yourself to feel bad for a time. The relentless pursuit of a perfect life will make you miserable. Express your hurts and upsets, and move on.

Focus points

✲ *Finding the time to focus on your goals is difficult.* Identify your 'prime time' – the chunks of time available to you each day. This is your most precious resource. Use it wisely.

✲ *Tracking your progress is vital.* Record the time you spend working on each task, or track the successes you have each day. Keep this visible, and accept the reality of your progress. Recognize when things are not working.

✻ It is healthy to express negative feelings, but misery can be as addictive as delay. After a reasonable amount of time, focus on the opportunities you have. Use the 'Spinning feelings' exercise to change the way you feel.

Having passion

You bought this book (or it was bought for you) because you struggle with procrastination. You now have tools to help you become more motivated. How will you use them? Will you pursue your dreams?

There will always be errands to run: bills need to be paid, calls need to be returned, and hassles need to be addressed. But such activities should not take over our lives. Take care of these things quickly, and you can focus on *the big stuff*.

We are sometimes oblivious to our purpose in life. The following exercise helps you see beyond the veil, and get in touch with your true values.

EXERCISE: IDENTIFY YOUR VALUES

▶ This exercise takes just a few minutes.

▶ The aim is to identify the key values you hold in life.

▶ When you have identified your values, keep them somewhere visible and look at them daily.

1 Read through the following checklist and write down any values that are important to you. Be honest with yourself – pick only those values you *truly* appreciate. Don't pick something because you think you *should* value it. Go with your initial feeling. Add any other values of your own.

▷ Acceptance	▷ Affection	▷ Belonging
▷ Accountability	▷ Authenticity	▷ Caring
▷ Achievement	▷ Balance	▷ Challenge
▷ Adventure	▷ Beauty	▷ Change

- Collaboration
- Commitment
- Compassion
- Competence
- Competition
- Confidence
- Contribution
- Cooperation
- Courage
- Creativity
- Curiosity
- Decency
- Decisiveness
- Development
- Discipline
- Efficacy
- Efficiency
- Empathy
- Excellence
- Enthusiasm
- Excitement
- Fairness
- Faith
- Flexibility
- Forgiveness
- Freedom
- Friendship
- Fun
- Generosity
- Gratitude
- Growth
- Happiness
- Health
- Honesty
- Honour
- Humility
- Humour
- Independence
- Influence
- Integrity
- Involvement
- Joy
- Kindness
- Knowledge
- Leadership
- Learning
- Love
- Loyalty
- Money
- Nature
- Openness
- Order
- Partnership
- Passion
- Patience
- Peace
- Play
- Possessions
- Prestige
- Progress
- Recognition
- Respect
- Responsibility
- Quality
- Security
- Service
- Sincerity
- Stability
- Status
- Success
- Teamwork
- Tolerance
- Tradition
- Trust
- Variety
- Wealth
- Wisdom

2 Now choose those values which *really* resonate. Think about the important moments in your life: Why were they valuable? What do you respect in others? What do you respect about yourself?

3 From your list of ten values, choose the six most important. Write them down, and pin them up next to your goal worksheet. Look at them every day.

4 Over time, you may feel like revising your list; this means you're finding out who you really are.

Did you identify your top six values? Reflect them in your actions, and you will be unstoppable. You will have *passion*.

'Lifestyle' procrastination

Next, think about your ambitions and dreams. If nothing could stop you, what would you achieve? Would you *create* or *build* something? Would you *do* or *teach* something? What would you want your obituary to say? Take a moment to answer these questions:

▶ 'Beyond caring for children and others, what is the most important thing I could be doing with my life?'

▶ 'Am I doing it?'

▶ 'If not, why not?'

Review your value list as you ask these questions. Unless you are focused on the most important things in life, you *are* procrastinating. You might think: 'But I have children, and debts, and errands to run, and a job to do.' And you would be right. You might even think: 'I don't have the time, the money, the resources, and the freedom I need. How can I work on these important things?' You would be right again. In this modern life our commitments, restrictions and limitations weigh heavily.

And yet, there is *always* something that can be done. Right at this moment, somebody somewhere is focused on something big – despite their limitations and restrictions. With a full-time job and a family to feed, perhaps you are not going to be *the next big thing* in Hollywood. But there are steps you can take to live your values. Before you turn your attention to excuses, accept your procrastination as the true problem.

Guilt holds us back, as does pessimism. We become overwhelmed by the enormity of the challenge. Busy lives drain us, and tiredness always exacerbates procrastination. However, progress can be made. Break huge and important goals into smaller targets, and make a start.

Your life is important. You owe it to your friends, your family, your children, and yourself to make the most of it. There must be balance, but neglecting your own needs is no more balanced than neglecting others. If you are happy, those who love you will share in it. This does not mean being selfish, but *irrational* guilt helps nobody.

Quick fix: Think big

To get anywhere, you will have to step out of your comfort zone. It is easy to keep yourself 'safe' by avoiding anxiety or stress. Unfortunately, you will procrastinate as a result.

Instead, whenever you see a genuine opportunity to do something – push yourself forward and take it. At such times, think to yourself: 'Just say yes! Just say yes! Just say yes!' Repeat this in your mind and seize the moment.

What are the most important things you *could* do with your life? Think big – you are only here once. Of course, there are always obstacles. But some are easier to deal with than others. Let's look at that now.

Good housekeeping

Even the best of us are overwhelmed sometimes. Bouncing back is important, but persistent difficulties are draining. Sometimes we need to 'clear the decks' before we can focus on the really important things.

To begin, consider the commitments in your life. When unwanted and unnecessary obligations drain your time, energy and passion – you need to cut them loose. Read through the following exercise, and identify the hassles you could do without.

EXERCISE: LETTING GO OF UNNECESSARY COMMITMENTS

▶ This exercise takes around five minutes.

▶ The aim is to identify and remove unwanted and unnecessary commitments.

▶ Use this exercise once or twice per year.

1 Write out a comprehensive list of the commitments you have in life. Consider those things which take time, effort, energy or concentration. Focus on the following:

▷ **Work:** Are there commitments incurred by your job? Especially note obligations that encroach on your free time, plus commitments you have for 'side projects'.

▷ **Family and children:** List all of the things you do for family members.

▷ **Community:** Are you involved in the local community? Note the obligations you have as a result.

▷ **Hobbies and online activity:** Are you a member of a group, club or sporting team? Do you participate in online forums? Make a note of the commitments you have here.

▷ **Home:** What must you do to keep your home life ticking over? List all of the commitments you have around the home, e.g. food shopping, cleaning, etc.

▷ **Health:** How do you stay fit and healthy? List these commitments as well.

Have we missed anything? Spend a good ten minutes listing everything you do on a regular or semi-regular basis. Be comprehensive.

2 Previously, you listed the six values you truly identify with. With that list to hand, go through each obligation written down so far and ask the following questions:

▷ 'How does this commitment improve my life and that of my family?'

▷ 'Do I have to do it? Can anybody else do it?'

▷ 'How would it affect my life if I stopped doing it?'

Be firm with yourself. Identify unnecessary commitments – one by one. Make plans to terminate them. Let your kids get the bus to school (they will cope). Stop going to that reading group you hate (they will survive). Stop running around after people just because you don't want to disappoint them (again, they will cope).

We often do things because we 'ought' to. Be honest with yourself: Do these obligations make you happier? Can you not simplify matters? Can you get somebody else to help?

You might think this is too easy, but it is really straightforward. Just say 'no'. Concentrate your efforts on doing a small number of things well, and you will achieve much more with your life.

LEARNING TO SAY 'NO!'
Learning to say 'no' is a key skill. Through fear, guilt and a desire to be kind or 'nice', we find ourselves agreeing to things we'd prefer not to do. Commitments pile up, as do our simmering resentments.

Saying 'no' *can* be straightforward. Whenever you are asked to do something, respond with one of these strategies:

▶ **Play for time.** Saying 'no' can lead to hurt feelings, hence your reluctance. Instead, point out the other things you need to do first. Can they get back to you in a month or so?

▶ **Consider a quid pro quo approach.** It does no harm to respond with: 'I've got a lot on. Could you to provide me with x, y and z – is that possible? Have a think about it and get back to me, perhaps?' Keep it balanced and fair, and this approach can lead to new opportunities in life.

▶ **Assert your boundaries.** If delaying or mutual back-scratching will not work, or when absolutely certain you want no part of it, a polite but firm can't. I have these other things I need to do' is your only option. Be calm and polite – and never apologize; time is your greatest resource. It should not be given away carelessly.

You may fear saying 'no' but it is easier than you imagine – old anxieties soon fall away. Removing unwanted commitments is important. By asserting your boundaries, you create time and conserve energy. Achieving your goals becomes easier.

Focus points

* *Identify your values and reflect them in your actions.* This will give you passion, and you will be unstoppable.

* *Your life is important.* Do something significant – whatever that might be. You needn't be selfish, but pay attention to your own needs as well as the needs of others.

* *We often do things because we 'ought' to.* Jettison unwanted and unnecessary obligations. Look at your life honestly and then simplify it.

* *Learning to say 'no' is important.* And, with just a little practice, it is easier than you imagine!

Clearing the decks

Once you have freed yourself from unnecessary commitments, turn your attention to other difficulties. Life *is* a series of problems, but we spend too much time ignoring them. The truth is, many of our problems can be solved quite easily.

Let's go through a quick list of typical *draining* situations. If you recognize any of the following problems, use your new skills to address them.

DE-CLUTTER YOUR HOME

Clutter accumulates over time, and multiplies when you're not looking. Is your house a zen-like garden of tranquillity, or are there piles of unsorted *stuff* everywhere? People who procrastinate tend towards the latter. Consider this approach:

▶ Be ruthless. Throw, sell or give away *anything* used less than three times in the past year. Go through shelves, cupboards, wardrobes, drawers, kitchen utensils, books, piles of *stuff*. If you do not use it, you do not need it.

▶ Buy three cardboard boxes via the Internet: one for things you need for a specific reason; one for things you cannot justify keeping; and a 'maybe' box (in case you decide to 'get back into' something).

▶ Seal the maybe box when finished. Write a deadline date, six to twelve months from now. When that date arrives, and if you have not opened the box, *then simply bin it or give it away, leaving it unopened*. You clearly do not need anything in this box!

This simple exercise makes a huge difference to people's lives. You could spend 15 minutes per day, tackle one room at a time, or dedicate a whole weekend to it. Where possible, enlist a friend to help you. And remember to be ruthless.

ADDRESS NIGGLING HEALTH CONCERNS

Getting older means accumulating aches and pains. We tend to wait until things become problematic before addressing them. However, taking care of niggling health issues makes a great difference to our lives.

▶ Are you carrying an injury? Do you need to fix a chipped tooth? Have you run into slight disrepair – not enough to cause significant difficulty, but enough to be noticeable? Are you generally run down?

▶ If so, write a list of health issues you'd like to address, and use the skills you have learned to tackle each one. Contact the appropriate professional without delay – you will appreciate the difference it makes.

DIET, EXERCISE AND SLEEP

People who procrastinate struggle to keep healthy. It *is* challenging to eat well, stay hydrated, exercise, and adopt healthy sleeping patterns. Many people struggle to fit exercise into their lives. However, with motivation you can turn your physical health around.

Healthy routines help us to overcome procrastination because our energy levels improve. Such goals are an excellent place to start; they are a foundation for future success.

Use the skills in this book to foster a healthier lifestyle – you will feel the benefits.

FAMILY PROBLEMS

Nothing disturbs our emotional wellbeing as much as conflict with family and close friends.

- We tolerate difficulties in our close relationships. And yet addressing these issues transforms lives. Can you talk to the person (or people) involved?

- Sometimes you need to compromise. There is no need to be a doormat, but do what you can to find peace – for the sake of your own emotional health.

- Of course, this not always possible. Sometimes there is nothing to be done – at which point, consider cutting your losses and freeing yourself of unwanted pain or negativity.

Some family situations just cannot be addressed. However, if there is anything you can do to resolve interpersonal conflicts, then take action. Life is too short.

NEGATIVITY FAST

As discussed previously, our thoughts affect our feelings and behaviours. If your head is full of *negative mental clutter*, you will struggle to perceive opportunities in life. Learning to recognize your thoughts as 'just thoughts' helps to maintain optimism and motivation.

- When you catch yourself thinking negatively – about yourself, about other people, about the past, about the future, or about the present moment – remind yourself: 'This is just a stupid thought.' It has no material value or worth; nor is it accurate, helpful or even correct.

- Remember, thoughts are just your *experience* of having a brain. You can choose which thoughts you believe, and which thoughts you discard. Be more tolerant – of yourself and others. With positivity comes motivation and hope.

Do you recognize anything on this list? Perhaps you have similar outstanding difficulties to address. If so, use your new skills and tackle anything which causes unhappiness. This should be a priority.

Pick one problem and take it as far as you can. This could mean establishing positive new habits, or taking care of long-standing situations. Then, choose a second problem and resolve it in a similar way. Do not try to fix everything all at once.

Within three to six months you could have more energy, happiness and determination. After a year or so, your life could be unrecognizable. There will always be *some* difficulty in life, but try to address any backlog. You'll then be ready to focus on the important things.

Complete the 'practice goal' you have been working towards – providing it is still relevant. Then, focus on your most pressing problems, and address them as best you can. Use the goal-setting process in Chapter 2. Life will feel better when you simplify it.

No matter which goals you work towards, remember to *track your progress*, *schedule tasks* and *bounce back from difficulties*. Then, turn your attention to doing something *amazing...*

Focus points

* *You may have outstanding issues in your life*; they tend to pile up because we procrastinate about them. Before focusing on the important things, draw up a list of the outstanding issues you can address.

* *Sorting out clutter makes a huge difference.* Buy three boxes – one for stuff to keep, one for stuff to sell or give away, and a 'maybe' box. Enlist the help of a friend, and be ruthless.

* *Do you have niggling health concerns?* If so, do not delay and contact an appropriate health professional. This will make a huge difference to your life.

* *Use the techniques in this book to foster healthy routines.* You will benefit directly, and the increased energy helps with procrastination.

* *Conflict with family or close friends can be emotionally debilitating.* If there is anything you can do to resolve such situations, take action – for your own benefit.

* *Our thoughts are just experiences generated by our brain.* You do not need to believe everything you think – be less negative and more tolerant. With positivity comes motivation and hope.

Setting big goals

When you have addressed the outstanding issues in your life, turn your attention to something *important*. Use the values identified earlier and enhance an area of your life. Perhaps one of these goals appeals:

▶ Improve your health and fitness.

▶ Establish an amazing relationship with a loving partner.

▶ Creating a network of satisfying friendships.

▶ Push your career to its limits.

▶ Retrain to do something you really want to do.

▶ Push your hobbies or interests as far as they will go.

▶ Develop a spiritual dimension to life.

▶ Create a wonderful home for you and your family.

In Chapter 1 you identified areas in your life where you procrastinate. Reread that checklist now. Which areas of your life do you need to focus on next? Think big. Choose something which leaves you feeling excited. Providing your goal reflects your values, this should not be a problem.

If you do struggle to feel excited about the possibilities, perhaps the problem lies with *goal conflict*.

GOAL CONFLICT

For example, imagine you want to retrain completely and embark upon a new career. Fantastic – this is one of the most important things you could do.

However, it could also lead to conflict. Perhaps you also hold the 'goal' of remaining comfortable in your current job. This second goal might be more of a feeling, but you cannot strive for something special and remain comfortable. There has to be some sacrifice.

There are certain things we *must* do. Pay the bills, insure the car, spend time with the children, and so on. But some things in life should not hold us back. A day job *is* just a day job.

Errands *are* just errands. Distractions *are* just distractions. Work towards something you will be remembered for, or you are procrastinating.

Achieving important goals requires *self-belief*. In Chapters 6 and 7 you learned how to negate limiting mindsets. This approach works well, and with practice your approach to life will become more optimistic. Limiting beliefs need not discourage you:

▶ Even the largest goal can be broken down into a number of steps.

▶ You can then tackle each step.

▶ Some steps may need to be repeated before you achieve your aims.

▶ However, providing you keep going, your success is *virtually* guaranteed.

When limiting beliefs take over, this logic is lost to fear and hesitation. Set big goals, plan them, track them, and bounce back from your setbacks. You will advance if you keep going.

HOW TO SET IMPORTANT GOALS

Setting huge goals is quite straightforward. Think of an important 'purpose' goal, and break it down into 'target' goals. For example:

▶ **Purpose goal:** Five years from now, graduate from university with a first-class degree.

▶ **Target goals:** Year 1 – clear my debts. Year 2 – clear more debt and switch to a part-time job. Years 3–5: enrol at university and pass each year with flying colours!

▶ **Year 1 immediate goals:** Draw up an accurate budget; cut monthly outgoings; set up direct debits to pay off debt more quickly; etc.

This example demonstrates how *purpose goals* can be broken into smaller *target goals* – which can be broken into smaller *immediate goals*. You would then use the full goal-setting process in Chapter 2.

All goals can be broken down into smaller steps, no matter how large they are. Avoid being overwhelmed by the enormity of the work involved by focusing on the immediate. *A journey of a thousand miles begins with a single step*. Behind the trite cliché lies a fundamental truth.

Quick fix: Carry out a daily review

At the end of each day, carry out a quick daily review. Look at your goals, your action plan, and the calendar, and assess the progress you have made. Ideally, spend some time tying up loose ends, and prepare for the following day.

Life can easily pass us by. Reviewing your progress daily counters this. It need only take five minutes, and you will feel more connected to your goals – and your life.

Summarizing goal-setting

In this chapter we have explored a framework for achieving the important things in life. Positive action inevitably involves challenge and difficulty, but success *is* possible. It just requires persistence.

HOW TO ACHIEVE ANY GOAL

Whatever goal you are focused on, follow this process.

1 Fully define your goal using the techniques in Chapter 2. If it will take more than a year to complete, break it down into several 'target goals'. If these 'target goals' will take more than a couple of months to complete, break them down further into 'immediate goals'.

2 Whatever your goals, break them down into *tasks*. Place those tasks in order, and you have an action plan (see Chapter 2).

3 Schedule your action plan by determining your 'prime time' for action (Chapter 10). As you hit these moments, consult your action plan and choose something to work on. Tackle the largest and most pressing tasks first.

4 For each task, write out a mini-action plan, detailing the steps you need to take. Determine how long these steps will take, and consider how you'll cope with procrastination urges (Chapter 5).

5 If you procrastinate – or think procrastination excuses – use the techniques in Chapter 5 to dismiss them.

6 If you feel reluctant to act, express your negative beliefs and ease past difficult emotions. Also, the 'Spinning negative emotions' technique is highly effective. Remember to stay relaxed. See Chapters 6 and 7 for more information.

7 Clear your mind, see the value of taking action and reduce the effort it takes to act. These approaches foster motivation (see Chapters 8 and 9).

8 Remember: delay is highly addictive. Your entire 'prime-time' slot could be wasted if you're not careful. Adopt a zero-tolerance approach to delay. This time is your most valuable resource. See Chapter 9 for more information.

9 Work on your mini-action plan for 45 minutes, acknowledging your success every 15 minutes or so. Reward yourself with a 15-minute break every hour or so.

10 Mark each 45-minute block on a visible calendar, and cross tasks off your action plan list as you complete them (Chapter 10).

Keep going until you have achieved your goal! You will need to attempt some tasks several times before making progress. You may need to learn new skills or ask somebody for help, but if you keep going – and if you bounce back when it gets difficult – you will make good progress.

This might seem too simple – but the techniques in this book can help you to achieve this, providing you keep practising them.

What goal will you focus on next? Are there problems you need to address, or a life-changing experience you want to pursue? Identify your prime time for action, schedule in a goal-setting session and get a plan together.

Focus points

* *Make sure your goal is visible*, preferably where you will see it daily.
* *Keep your action plan next to it.* If there are steps you prefer to keep private, it is OK to leave them off your list.
* *Have your prime-time slots printed out as well.* Get to know them off by heart.
* *Include a printed calendar with your goal.* Track your progress, and adjust your efforts as required.

Having the confidence to start

Sometimes people think: 'I *will* do this. Just when I have the confidence.' But confidence only comes from *taking action*. Consider these important points:

▶ Waiting to feel confident does not improve confidence. It can *only* improve by taking action.

▶ You will rarely meet a champion without a coach.

▶ You have good qualities and deserve some success in life.

If you are waiting to feel confident before tackling life head on, you are in for a long wait. Taking action is the *only* way you'll improve your confidence. It is vital to understand this. Start small and build things up. Then your confidence will grow.

To limit procrastination, seek support from others and be accountable in return. Even elite athletes have their team behind them: coaches, fitness experts, sports psychologists and so on. As a general rule, we perform best when we're connected to other people.

Whatever you're trying to achieve in life, ask yourself: 'Am I isolated?' Do you have a mentor? A cheerleader? A coach? Are there groups, networks or societies you can connect with? To whom can you be accountable to? What support can you gain? At the very least, share your goals with trusted friends, and find local groups where you can put your new skills to good use.

You deserve some happiness in life. No matter what mistakes you have made, everyone deserves the opportunity to do something important. At the earliest opportunity, complete the following exercise.

EXERCISE: ACCEPTING YOUR GOOD POINTS

▶ This exercise takes just five minutes.

▶ The aim is to understand (and accept) that other people view you differently.

1 Ask a (trusted) friend to write down five things they like, respect or love about you. If they would like, do the same in return.

2 When you get the list, accept the reality of it. Their view is clearer than your own, despite what you might think.

3 Keep the list safe, and refer to it once per day for the next month or so.

It is a simple exercise – have no fear of it and do not procrastinate. Gain an insight into the way others perceive you, and accept that reality. Your motivation will improve when you recognize your good points.

Moving on

And that's it. You have the insights, the tools and the techniques you need to achieve your goals.

This may take weeks, months or even longer. It will not always be straightforward, and we cannot get everything right first time. Remember to track your progress and bounce back from disappointment. Keep going, and your success is virtually guaranteed.

Bear in mind you are still *learning* to overcome procrastination. Mastering the skills in this book takes months, and they require constant use to stay fresh. Procrastination can never be completely eradicated, but you can motivate yourself to achieve your goals and change your life.

So – keep practising. Use your new skills to counter *denial*, *refusal* and *delay* as much as possible. Dismiss excuses and ease past negative feelings. See the value in taking action, and mitigate the effort required. And most of all, remember: although not a robot, you are capable of achieving something amazing. Good luck.

Index